GEORGIA
Through the Looking Glass

Caleb Pirtle III

TRAVELINK PUBLISHING COMPANY
Dallas—Waxahachie—Atlanta

Published for TraveLink Publishing Company's "Portrait of America Travel Series" under the direction of:

Executive Editor—Caleb Pirtle III
Director of Communications—Ed Stone
Marketing Director—Collinson, Mischik, & Associates of
    Atlanta, Georgia
    Newt Collinson
    Larry Mischik
    Karen Hoey
Marketing Associate—Empire Publishing of Dallas, Texas
    Mike Shaw
    Glenn Shaw

Art & Design, Charter Art, Arlington, Texas
Typography—Danny Pope, Waxahachie, Texas

Library of Congress Cataloging-in-Publication Data

Pirtle III, Caleb, 1941-

GEORGIA THROUGH THE LOOKING GLASS
1. Title

ISBN: 0-929505-00-X
Library of Congress Catalog Number: 88-50583

Manufactured in the United States of America

First Printing

Contents

Dedicated to Hanna Ledford, Director of the Tourist Division, Deputy Commissioner of the Georgia Department of Industry & Trade, and to her fine staff, who have all worked so diligently, so creatively, and so efficiently to make Georgia one of America's top travel destination states:

Harvey Monk, Assistant Director
Gary Womack, Director of Advertising
Ginger Taylor, Georgia Tourism Product Development
Karin Koser, Public Relations Manager

The Winds Of Pride Come Blowing Through Georgia

The old man hitched up his bib-overalls and leaned back against an old oak tree that was as gnarled and weather-beaten as his own face. He closed his eyes for a moment, smiled as he thought of the world around him, then whispered softly:

"Georgia? Why, it's a grand and glorious place, son. It's got a little bit of everything. You can wake up with the wind from its mountains blowin' hard in your face, and if you keep headin' south, you can be leavin' your footprints in the sands by the Atlantic Ocean before the day ever gets around to chasin' the sun from the sky. I'll tell you one thing, son, and you can hang onto it like gospel, which is what it is. If Georgia ain't got it, then you ain't got no reason to want it."

1

1.

The echoes from many voices have drifted down the long, winding backroads of Georgia.

Sharp as a gunshot in the hollows of its high country.

Soft as a southern wind in its pines.

A whisper where the sands become white, then wet, and are sometimes stolen by the ragged fingers of a restless sea.

The voices have talked of love.

Their words have been the music of laughter.

They have been steeled with anger.

And often they were stilled by sadness.

But always the voices have spoken with a touch of pride that boils up from deep within the bosom of Georgia itself.

A respected architect said of its grand, monumental old homes: "Nowhere did the Greek Revival produce a more perfect blending of the dignified and the gracious, the impressive and the domestic, than in the lovely houses of the 1830s and 1840s of upstate Georgia."

And William Makepeace Thackery, on a visit to Savannah in 1856, stayed at the Andrew Low home, and he was visibly impressed with what could be built by wealth gleaned from Georgia's fabled cotton fields. He noted that the handsome brick and stucco house, with an iron balcony, was easily "the most comfortable quarters I have ever had in the United States. They are tremendous men, these cotton merchants."

Fanny Kemble, a gifted English actress who became an author after the acrid smoke cleared from the War Between the States, walked the silent sands of her St. Simons Island home, and she described its beauty as "a salt marsh upon a raised causeway that was perfectly alive with land crabs. The sides of this road across the swamp were covered with a thick and close embroidery of creeping moss or rather lichens of the most vivid green and red; the latter made my horse's path look as if it were edged with an exquisite pattern of coral. It was like a thing in a fairy tale."

William McIntosh, head chieftain of the Cowetan Indians, too, loved the land he called home. But in 1825 he saw it swiftly slipping from the grasp of his people, and he knew that his time on Georgia soil was growing short.

At first his words were edged with anger: "The White man is growing in the state of Georgia; he wants our lands; he will buy them now, but by and by he will take them and the little band of our people will be left to wander without homes, poor, despised and beaten like dogs."

Then came the farewell words of sadness as he turned to trek a trail of tears toward a new, strange territory beyond the Mississippi: "The day is come when we surrender this country of our forefathers, land of our nativity, our home. Our people seek new lands. Our heart remains."

The white man came and took what the Indian had always called his own.

Land. And gold.

Up in the Georgia mountains, old Bony Tank loved to lure prospectors to his land—salted with gold dust fired from a shotgun. If necessary, Tank simply stuffed his chaw of tobacco with gold, then spit the flakes into the pan before handing it to another speculator. Tank sold a lot of land that way.

One man told him, "With your talent for finding gold and my money, we could get rich in Africa." Tank thought it was worth a try. But when he arrived at the edge of the ocean, he simply shook his head and said, "That little pond's up, and I'm not crossin' it till it goes down. I'm going on back to where I belong." And he went back to the hills of Auraria.

Wisdom has always come out of rural Georgia like spilled moonshine.

"You can always tell there's a storm comin' if the cats and rats play after sundown," old timers would say.

Or they might add, "When fires commence to spittin', there'll soon be a fall of right heavy snow."

Farmers, after a hard day of plowing, have been known to yell, "I'm so hungry I could eat a bull and it a bellerin'."

And moonshiners saw no harm at all in their brew. "It's not agin' the Bible," they swore, "it's just agin' the law."

Somebody, it seemed, was always breaking the law of the land. War came, an unholy and uncivil war, and it raged madly across Georgia.

Homes burned brightly in the night. Cities lay in ashes. An old land held new graves. General William T. Sherman was marching to the sea.

Union Major Henry Hitchcock, gazed upon the November ruins of Atlanta, and he wrote: "This P.M. the torch applied, also sundry buildings blown up by shells inside. Clouds of heavy smoke rise and hang like a pall over the doomed city. At night the grandest and most awful scene. Half the horizon shows immense and raging fires, lighting up the whole heaven. First, bursts of smoke, dense black volumes, then tongues of flame, then huge waves of fire roll up into the sky. Now and then are heavy explosions and as one fire sinks another rises farther along the horizon...a line of fire and smoke, lurid, angry, dreadful to look upon."

Sherman said simply, "A spirit of exhilaration runs through the entire army."

But a Georgia mother could only whisper, as she wiped the dampness from her eyes, "We are cut off from the world."

A Confederate commander stood painfully and glanced at an urgent dispatch he had received from a beleaguered officer at the front. It read: "I am facing a superior force in my front, on my right, and on my left flank. What shall I do?"

The commander sighed and wrote back: "Fight 'em."

It was too little. It was much too late.

But, as an old Appalachian Mountain farmer always said: "Three of a kind can beat two pair. And four of a kind can beat a full house. But nothing on earth can beat a good try."

Georgia has never been afraid to try, regardless of the odds that might be stacked against it.

It has withstood the cannons of war.

It has risen from its own ashes.

With pride.

And defiance.

Strong.

Yet as gentle as the winds that ruffle through its dogwood and cherry and azalea blossoms, as noble and aristocratic as the aging, scarred white columns of its antebellum homes.

They are the glory of the past.

Theirs are the classic faces of Georgia, distinctive and unbowed, found in high country and upon the Piedmont plains, veiled by the pines and a salt mist from the sea, legacies that grew out of the power and the kingdom of cotton.

They, like the echoing words, remain.

Proud.

And memorable.

And unforgotten, never to be forgotten.

4

COLONIAL COAST

''The creeks overflow: a thousand rivulets run
'Twixt the roots of the sod; the blades of the marshgrass stir;
Passeth a hurrying sound of wings that westward whir;
Passeth, and all is still; and the currents cease to run;
And the sea and the marsh are one.''

—Sidney Lanier
The Marshes of Glynn

5

The surf of the Atlantic beckons to the
playground of the Golden Isles.

2.

$\mathcal{I}$t all looks so peaceful now, down where the sea ends its Atlantic journey and crawls at last onto the barrier sands of the Golden Isles.

It is quiet. And undisturbed.

The marshes of Glynn glisten in the last glow of a fading sunlight, as the shadows of evening fall in splinters from the gnarled, aging limbs of a live oak tree.

A sea gull reaches out to catch the wind. The tides take the last footprint from the foam of a ragged surf line. From St. Marys, a ferry follows the whitecaps back from the national seashore of Cumberland Island, back from beaches unspoiled and unchanged by the ages. The faint image of a shrimp boat, hurrying to beat the night home to Brunswick, is merely a pen and ink sketch outlined against a purple sky. The isles are at peace with themselves and with the sea around them.

But once their sands ran red with blood. They shuddered while Georgia was being birthed amidst the awful sound of pain and gunfire. Men fought to hold onto the coastal plain. Men died to take it away. And not even time has been able to remove the traces that their days of battle left behind.

$\mathcal{I}$t was to the shoreline of the Golden Isles where James Oglethorpe came in 1733 to build his foundation on soil that would become the nation's thirteenth colony. Unfortunately, the French and Spanish already claimed the land. Oglethorpe promptly built Fort Frederica, Britain's main fortification on the Southern frontier. He knew that trouble was on its way.

War struck St. Simons Island, loud and fierce.

And at the battle of Bloody Marsh, Oglethorpe's soldiers, badly

7

outnumbered, ambushed the horde of Spanish troops and drove them back to the sea. It was the last moment of glory for Fort Frederica. The British regiment was soon disbanded, and only an empty wind blew across the walls of an empty fort. In 1758 a major fire virtually destroyed it all.

The National Park Service still offers self-guided tours through the ruins of both the outpost and the town that had grown up around it. The fort itself has been reduced in size by the elements, by erosion, and a brick and tabby tower is the only remnant of the barracks that once were the home for two hundred soldiers. A visitor's center houses a museum with exhibits taken from excavations of the historic bluff.

Savannah had its own mud, stone, and brick sentinels to fight its own battles, vigilant guardians of the gracious living that was found within its array of grand old homes.

Fort Jackson was there at the beginning, standing strong during the Revolutionary War, the War of 1812, and the War Between the States. Even now, serving as a Maritime Museum, it is still on the job, guarding a part of Georgia's past.

Down the road, Fort Pulaski, Confederate military leaders believed, was invincible. It had been Robert E. Lee's first engineering assignment after receiving his commission from West Point. And nothing was stronger. Nothing nor no one could destroy it. But some military genius had invented a big new gun that nobody in the South knew about. And from its mount on Hilton Head Island, so far away, that big new gun almost blew the invincible walls of Pulaski off the face of the earth. Today the restoration is a beautifully landscaped historic site, operated by the National Park Service. Peace, it seems, always does wonders for forts.

At Darien is the historic site of Fort King George, an Indian village and Spanish mission that became the most southerly outpost of all the British colonies. The Military Museum at Hinesville's Fort Stewart, traces the glory, the agony of war from 1860 to the present, exhibiting weapons, flags, uniforms, and firearms. Fort McAllister at Richmond Hill served as a key earthwork fortification in defense of Savannah, back when Union warships bombarded the coast. Near Midway, a visitor's center stands upon the battered shoreline of Georgia's second largest Colonial seaport, showcasing the heritage of the earthen Fort Morris, scarred by Revolutionary War shot, and the last, but unforgotten, town of Sunbury. Fort Screven, manned during the Spanish-American War, has been the lone sentry of Tybee Island since 1875. And not far from Savannah, Wormsloe is the 1736 country estate of one of the first colonists to settle Georgia. Pathways at the historic site lead past crumbling tabby ruins of the fortifications and earthworks at Fort Wimberly.

The winds of war no longer disturb the golden sands of the Golden Isles.

But their memories remain, proud and unforgotten, never to be forgotten.

*he beaches of the Golden Isles are lost
n the silence of their own solitude.

A Gentle and Genteel Way of Island Life

The Marshes of Glynn were poet Sidney Lanier's country. He would sit and listen to the coming of the tide, watching the ever-changing golds and greens that sunlight and shadow painted across that vast wind-rippled ocean of marsh grass.

And Sidney Lanier wrote:

> *Ye marshes, how candid and simple*
> *and nothing-withholding and free*
> *Ye publish yourselves to the sky and*
> *offer yourselves to the sea·*

But time changes all things. And the isles of Jekyll, St. Simon, Little St. Simon, and Sea Island—all sprawling beneath the graying Spanish moss beards of antique oaks—are far different than they were in the days when Lanier tracked the lonely solitude of their rolling dunes, captivated by the primitive beauty of the land around him, understanding of the historical legacy that lay sometimes in ruin upon the sand. Only the Marshes of Glynn remain unchanged.

Georgia's collection of barrier Isles have tempted and taunted mankind since the 1500s when adventurers, adrift in a strange, new world, came wading ashore in search of gold. Instead, they found nature unspoiled and undisturbed, its broad expanse of marshes and beaches all awash in the golden glow of a fading sunlight. With awe and reverence, they would forever refer to the ground beneath their feet as the Golden Isles. The Spanish claimed it. The British came and took it away, leaving the sands stained crimson at the Battle of Bloody Marsh. In time, there arose rumors of stolen Pirate treasure buried amidst the dunes. Great, prosperous rice and cotton plantations were carved out of gnarled oak thickets. And the isles became a hideaway for America's millionaires who once proclaimed, "No unwanted foot ever touched the island." Now, all feet are welcome where sands are golden, and the Marshes of Glynn reach out and offer themselves to the sea.

The Golden Isles are anchored to the mainland by a series of causeways that connect them to the Victorian port city of Brunswick. Old Town Brunswick is a portrait of antiquity, its streets and squares laid out long before the Revolutionary War and named for members of English royalty and nobility. Between Gloucester and Prince Streets, for example, are the home docks for a fleet of colorful boats that helped Brunswick earn its title as the shrimp capital of the World.

But no longer does Brunswick depend solely on the sea for survival. Now, its lifeline is tied squarely to the length and the breadth of the Golden Isles, where golf and tennis are played against a backdrop of crumbling historical ruins, and there are intriguing museums and grand old mansions to explore, all surrounded by miles of gentle beaches that lead quietly on down to the golden-tipped Marshes of Glynn.

The beach is awash in the golden glow of a setting sun.

10

Perhaps that is why the Intersection of I-95 and U.S. 341 at Brunswick is clustered with eleven motels that collectively have 1,200 rooms, all within easy walking distance from sixteen restaurants, all only fifteen minutes away from the beckoning sands of the isles themselves.

St. Simons Island has a quiet beauty that is almost melancholy. It hears the laughter. It heard the mourning for those died when the land was a wilderness, then a battleground, then filled with the graves of those who had fallen. St. Simons is the largest of the Golden Isles, roughly the size of Manhattan, virtually hidden behind the Spanish moss that dangles from its legendary live oaks. In fact, back in 1794, many of the hardy oaks were cut from Gascoige Bluff and used to build the famous U.S. frigate, *Constitution*, a ship nicknamed "Old Ironsides" simply because the wood was that strong and that tough and that impenetrable.

St. Simons clings to a gentle way of life where nothing is rushed, and the memories of its sometimes grand, sometimes turbulent past lie amidst the remnants of weathered, decaying plantations, churchyard cemeteries, and the national monument at Fort Frederica, built by General James Oglethorpe to defend the Southern frontier against Spanish attack. It stood strong and defiant when the raging battle finally came, and a hundred Spanish soldiers lost their lives and left their blood to dry upon the unwavering Marshes of Glynn. The brick and tabby ruins of the fort stand proud, with ancient cannons guarding the pathway toward a visitor's center.

When Oglethorpe arrived in 1736, he brought with him his chaplain, John Wesley, and a secretary, Charles Wesley. The Wesley brothers, who would one day lead the Methodist movement across America, preached their first sermon to the "murderous, gluttonous Indians" under a giant oak where peaceful little Christ Church now stands. It was built in 1884, replacing the original church that had been destroyed by Union soldiers who cooked and slept inside the sanctuary during the War Between the States. Gone, too, is the original lighthouse of 1811 that once towered as the lone sentinel of the Georgia coast, blown up by retreating Confederate troops who did not want Northern invaders using the beacon to guide Federal ships into the chain of islands. The present-day lighthouse, erected in 1872, houses the exhibits of the Museum of Coastal History.

Few places notched along the eastern seaboard can match the quiet beauty or the historical significance that pervades the sanctity of the island. It's no wonder that—just before the turn of the century—St. Simons gained fame as a resort area. The *summer people* would arrive by boat, then climb aboard horse-drawn surreys for a quick ride to seasonal hotels and boarding houses. It seems that St. Simons Island, as the decades passed, has always been able to successfully blend its fragile, primitive environment with a fascinating

A silent cannon guards the ruins of Fort Frederica.

13

collection of beachfront villas and vacation cottages. And now the isle also has a whole new set of luxury condominiums and top resort facilities—such as those found at the urbane and elegant Beach Club, King and Prince, Sea Gate Inn, Country Hearth Inn, and Sea Palms.

Eighty-one holes of golf have been sculptured through oak alleys and alongside the delicate salt marshes, tidal rivers, and expansive beaches that catch the wayward Atlantic winds. However, there are hazards on St. Simons that are uncommon to most championship courses. At Sea Palms, one golfer slammed his drive to the edge of a lake on No. 18. And as he stood calmly to address his next shot, a crab reached up out of the water, grabbed the ball, and raced away. Sea Palms is still trying to figure out a fair and equitable ruling.

Such is life on the Golden Isles.

Sea Island is interwoven with a reverent air of opulence that has been fashioned by the Cloister, the grande dame of Southern resorts. Its Spanish-Mediterranean architecture, a touch of the Old World, is draped by the tropical umbrella of palms and magnolias and huge oaks, tinseled with Spanish moss.

Sea Island was nothing more than an undeveloped marsh and goat pasture when Howard Coffin, automobile and aviation pioneer, first purchased the old Retreat Plantation and five miles of beach back in 1925.

His plan was simple enough. There were many wealthy and powerful people, Coffin knew, who had always wanted to own a piece of their own island. He would make their dream possible, selling them a parcel of land and, if necessary, selling them a home as well. The grand hotel he built beside the beach of Sea Island was only a temptation, a promise of the good life, the cloistered life that could be uncovered by all who came to leave their footprints upon the sands of the Golden Isles.

But, alas, the blues of the great depression struck the country. Coffin suddenly found himself broke, and he placed the Cloister under the guidance of his nephew, Alfred Jones. It was a wise decision. Jones recalled, "We started as a real estate development company, but nobody was buying land. So we discovered ourselves in the resort business."

In time, the Cloister became a legend, a way of life for noted figures in the world of business, a place of leisure and luxury that became a home away from home for the quiet set, the genteel, the financial aristocracy who sometimes wrote wills, leaving their reservations to their children.

The resort's 27-hole golf course, located on St. Simons Island, winds around a series of lakes, inlets, and lagoons that once surrounded the antebellum Retreat Plantation. The drive to the clubhouse, a restoration of the plantation tabby corn barn, is lined by twin rows of live oaks planted in the 1830s. And beside the par 4, No. 1 tee crumbles the red brick ruins of the historic old Retreat itself, now bound together by climbing vines.

Golf is played amidst the lush terrain of the Golden Isles.

15

The Cloister also offers fishing in the surf or inland waterway, a skeet range at the Sea Island Gun Club, ten tennis courts, a riding stable with fine-gaited trail horses, boating in a custom-made cruiser, and hunting for either quail or the elusive marsh hens that abound in the tidal grasses.

To Sea Island have come four generations of the rich, the famous, the important, the powerful.

Many have never left, building their own opulent cottages amidst the tropical blooms of Sea Island Drive, known far and wide as Millionaire's Row.

Once the millionaires came to Jekyll Island, back when it was an exclusive and private club, linked to the mainland only by boat. In those years, members stayed at the Club House, a 60-room, four-story masterpiece of Victorian architecture that had been built in 1887. It was an era when such families as the Rockefellers and Vanderbilts and Morgans all gathered for hunting, golf, lawn parties, and horseback riding, ultimately building cottages that looked more like mansions.

On a January day in 1915, many of them sat rigidly in the Club House with Theodore N. Vail, then president of AT&T, and watched him dial the first transcontinental call ever made in the United States. The connection brought him the voices of Alexander Graham Bell in New York, Bell's assistant in San Francisco, and President Woodrow Wilson in Washington, D.C.

The Jekyll Island Club voted to close during World War II and was never reopened. The state purchased the isle in 1947 for $675,000 and began developing it as a public resort. And recently the historic old Club House underwent a $16.6 million rehabilitation that restored its original glory, transforming it into a fine hotel that once again captures the lifestyle of a fabulous era that has dimmed but is not forgotten. Numerous other accommodations are located on the beach side of Jekyll.

One of the Golden Isles reflects a quiet solitude that has not been spoiled by the changing times.

Little St. Simons is a 10,000-acre barrier isle that has more than six miles of undeveloped, untrammaled Atlantic Ocean beach. Accessible by a short boat ride across coastal rivers and up tidal creeks, it has been preserved and protected for almost a century as a family retreat, complete with an old 1916 hunting lodge that offers accommodations for only two dozen guests. It offers family-style meals and fireside chats with resident naturalists who can tell you all about the island's 300 species of birds, alligators, and Indian shell mounds. It's a place to fish, camp, hike, take horseback rides, or explore six miles of barren beach. The English actress and author Fanny Kemble once lived here, and she wrote of the "wild savage loneliness" she felt on the isle.

Perhaps no other description is necessary down where the Marshes of Glynn bend forward in the wind and touch the sea.

Old Christ Church on St. Simons Island occupies the site where John and Charles Wesley preached their first sermon on American soil.

17

Long Ago Haunt of the Rich

There was a haunting quality about Jekyll Island, far removed from the madding crowds. Golden marshes bent gently in the winds, and restless dunes were sometimes caressed and sometimes battered by the unpredictable tides of the Atlantic. It was a place of retreat, a place where secrets could be kept hidden behind those veils of Spanish moss that hung mysteriously from its gnarled and ancient live oak trees. And Jekyll Island beckoned to the rich, the very, very rich.

For the Indians, Jekyll had been home. For buccaneers who plundered the eastern shoreline, it was a refuge. But as the 19th century grew to a close, Jekyll's sands were marked by the footprints of the wealthiest families in America, all looking for a hideaway where they could escape and find a measure of freedom from social climbers and a probing press.

On April 4, 1886 the Jekyll Island Club was formed, and the *New York Times* boldly predicted that it was "going to be the *creme de la creme* of all." So from the North they came, bringing such Midas-touch names as Astor, Rockefeller, Pulitzer, Gould, Vanderbilt, Goodyear, and Morgan, fifty-three members who collectively owned a sixth of the world's wealth. They were men in the midst of transforming America from an agrarian society to an industrial world power, and they all wanted a secluded place within a 24-hour train excursion, or a leisurely boat ride, from New York. They found it on the smallest of Georgia's historic Golden Isles.

During the next 40 years, fifteen Victorian and Edwardian retreats were built on the isle. They were called cottages, although some had as many as 25 to 31 rooms. And one had a total of seventeen bathrooms. In addition, the millionaires fashioned one of the finest golf courses in the country, as well as tennis courts and indoor and outdoor swimming pools.

It was luxury at its finest. But even luxury fell on hard times. During World War II, supplies and labor became too difficult to find, so the millionaires closed their doors on the island in '42 and never opened them again.

Five years later, Georgia bought Jekyll's scenic acres, and it became a playground that the very, very rich had only dreamed about, stretching for ten miles along the Atlantic and spilling back among the dunes and palms. The isle is a year-round retreat for sailing, fishing, tennis, bicycling, and 63 holes of gold, including some holes built by the millionaire's club almost a century ago. Jekyll's beaches, anchored by fine hotels, rank with the best on the coast.

Also, the Jekyll Island Authority has carefully recreated that distinctive era of gingerbread trim, of piazzas and porte cocheres. The historic club house has been rehabilitated and reopened as a hotel. And the Jekyll Island Museum operates and offers tours through many of the grand mansions where the highest of America's high society once gathered to hammer out so many of the legendary deals that reshaped their country.

The Crane House reflects the good life of Jekyll Island's history.

19

A City of Great Expectations, A City of the Ages

Savannah has always been the most sought after of cities, a somewhat sophisticated, somewhat elegant portrait of the Greek Revival, Gothic, and Romanesque South that grew up around walled courtyards and oak-shaded squares, graced by a touch of architectural nobility at the edge of the sea.

It was destined for greatness, even from the beginning, the refined and polished creation of General James Oglethorpe who, on a February day in 1733, led a band of 120 British settlers ashore at Yamacraw Bluff to establish an unrelenting foothold on a land that would become the last of the thirteen original colonies.

Savannah, at the skilled hands of Oglethorpe, became the nation's first planned city. He immediately proceeded to lay out the blocks, lots, and public squares, carefully designing the symmetrical patterns that would one day give Savannah its aesthetic and unmistakable appearance.

A description of Savannah, written three years later, said, "The lots are fenced in...Their houses are built at a pretty large distance from one another, for fear of fire; the streets are very wide, and there are great squares left at proper distances, for markets and other conveniences."

Savannah thus became a city of great expectations, and it has fulfilled most of them.

Savannah, through the years, has been both inspired and influenced by the odd mixture of nationalities who came to build their hopes, their dreams, and their homes beneath the Spanish moss that enshrouded its wide streets. There were English Anglicans, Presbyterians from the Scottish Highlands, Sephardic Jews of Spanish and Portuguese descent, Moravians, Lutheran Salzburgers, Irish Catholics, Huguenots, French Protestants, and West Africans, slaves, who, in time, spread a unique Gullah culture among the sea islands.

The sea became Savannah's one link to prosperity, and prosperity was Savannah's inheritance in the new land. By 1735, the city was a flourishing seaport, even exporting silk to Europe, although its ultimate fortune would come from those never-ending fields of cotton that kept ships sailing toward Yamacraw Bluff as fast as they could get there.

Savannah, however, was different. So were its wealthy planters. They did not construct great plantation houses out upon their land where cotton stalks clustered thick and white. Instead, they built their manors down upon the squares of Savannah, and their riches were reflected in the Greek Revival, Gothic, and Romanesque architecture that became their homes.

But time has an unfortunate way of changing things, and it wasn't particularly kind to Savannah. The centuries began to take their toll. The city was left scarred by bullets, by age, by neglect, and finally by decay. Remnants of the good life were left in ruin. But Savannah never lost its pride.

Savannah has been influenced and inspired by its people and by its river.

In fact, it gloried in its past miseries. After all, there were the tragic fires of 1796 and 1820, the battles of Revolutionary War that stormed through its streets, and the War Between the States that brought death, destruction, and the feared General William T. Sherman all marching to its door steps.

The contemporary city of Savannah, perhaps, is proudest of the one war it did win, the one it fought so defiantly against architectural deterioration that, by the 1950s, was running rampant down its streets. Mansions had become slums. Many were being demolished. Other fine old homes simply sat empty with their beams sagging and rotting away. And residents were turning their backs on Savannah's stylish but antique downtown area. For thirty years, there had been attempts to cut through the squares, which had become nothing but bare patches of dirt, rip up parks, distort Oglethorpe's old city plan, and abandon, even tear down, the buildings which had made Savannah so distinctive. The people of Savannah had lost interest in their past, in the legacy that Oglethorpe's colonists had left them.

As early as the 1920s and 30s, the National Park Service had brought a sense of architectural restoration to Savannah when it pieced back together the ruins of Fort Pulaski. Then in the 1940s, work began to restore Trustees Garden, the 1734 site of the first agricultural experimental garden in North America. In that ten-acre plot, early-day farmers cultivated and nurtured trees, herbs, and plants from around the world, trying to discover just what would work in that rich Georgia soil. And what they liked best were cotton and peaches, which became the foundation for the Georgia argicultural industry.

In 1954, Savannah lost its historic Old City Market, a huge rambling building on Ellis Square where farmers in wagons and carts for decades had brought their fresh harvest of fruit and vegetables. The demolition made some people mad. It awoke others. And a new interest in Savannah's decaying architectural heritage was rekindled throughout the city.

Suddenly the wrecking ball was aimed squarely at the Davenport House, one of the South's most handsome examples of Georgian architecture. Seven ladies promptly formed the Historic Savannah Foundation, stepped forward, and refused to let the Davenport House be cleared away and replaced by a funeral home parking lot. They literally stayed the wrecker's hand just twenty-four hours before demolition was to begin. Their efforts formed the genesis of Savannah's self preservation.

Volunteers went from door to door and found 1,100 buildings that were classified as notable, excellent, or exceptional. Work on them became an integral part of Savannah's daily life, and more than a thousand of the structures have undergone renovation. The twenty town squares are

Savannah has long been known for its beautiful homes and gracious hospitality.

landscaped gardens with monuments and fountains. And a 2.5 square mile of Savannah forms the nation's largest urban historic district, a site of "exceptional value in commemorating or illustrating the history of the United States."

Bicycle and walking tours lead down quaint streets that link the best of all ages in the city. Take Madison Square, for example. To the West is the Green-Meldrim Mansion, used by Sherman for his headquarters when the Union army took hold of Savannah. It was from this manor that the Union general sent Abe Lincoln his famous message: "I beg to present you as a Christmas gift the city of Savannah with 150 heavy guns and plenty of ammunition and also about 25,000 bales of cotton." To the East is the Jewett House, visited often by Robert E. Lee while he was commanding the Confederate coastal defenses. Not far away is the birthplace and home of Juliette Gordon Low who in 1912 founded the Girl Scouts. The house itself became Savannah's first registered landmark and, like the Davenport and Green-Meldrim Houses, is open to the public.

Other historic homes function as museums as well. The Andrew Low House played host to both Robert E. Lee and William Makepeace Thackery. The William Scarbrough House was home for a merchant and promoter of the first steamship to cross the Atlantic. The King Tisdale cottage preserves the black history and culture of Savannah and the sea islands. The Owens-Thomas house holds rare furnishings that were the handiwork of American cabinetmakers in the early nineteenth century. Its walled garden has many plants found in American gardens during that era. And the Telfair Academy of Arts and Sciences, the oldest public art museum in the South, contains a superb collection of American and European paintings and sculpture.

The restorations have given Savannah its aristocratic image back, but it is down along Rousakis Riverfront Plaza where the good times roll. What were once cotton warehouses have been converted into places of food and entertainment. At the Pirate's House, for example, meals are served with tales of the sea, including one that says the buccaneer who inspired Treasure Island's Long John Silver actually died withing the dwelling. The warehouses of nearby Factor's Walk have undergone a similar transformation and hold restaurants, taverns, specialty shops, and the Ships of the Sea Museum.

Horse-drawn carriages meander along avenues lined with moss-draped oaks and Victorian houses. Cap'n Sam's riverboat cruises the Savannah River. The guns are silenced at Forts Jackson, McAllister, Screven, and Pulaski, once believed to be an impregnable blockade of the river.

Savannah is what it was meant to be, a historical showplace to be remembered, a city of the ages.

Okefenokee Swamp

A Primitive Wilderness, The Land of Trembling Earth

The Seminoles found a refuge, but never really a home, in a great swampland of black water and giant cypress where only the brave dared venture after dark. They walked upon the marshes and felt the ground quake nervously beneath their footsteps, and, with fear and respect, they whispered its name: "Okefenokee," the land of trembling earth.

It is a jungle, a primitive wilderness of plant and animal that many believe has become "America's greatest natural botanical garden."

Okefenokee's Swamp Park at Waycross provides access to a world that, its tour guides say, is one of the quietest, most peaceful places known to mankind, especially in those last, darkening moments just before sundown. The trembling earth seems to be a mysterious landscape without end, stretching far beyond the spreading lilly pads, the brown prairies of saw grass and hammocks, the stark cypress trees that are festooned with the graying beards of Spanish moss.

In reality, the Okefenokee is a vast peat bog filling a huge, but shallow, depression that once was part of an ancient sea. The swamplands cover about 412,000 acres—more than 600 square miles—and their stained waters form the source of both the St. Mary's and Suwanee Rivers.

Alligators and snakes hide away there. And so do deer, raccoons, otters, bobcats, and the black bear. But it is the constant croaking of the frogs that keep the swamp awake at night. Great blue and green herons soar overhead. Osprey and white egrets thread the narrow channels in flight. Even the rare pileated woodpeckers have come to the Okefenokee to make one of their final stands for survival.

The bayous, the bays, the lakes reflect the vibrant and ever-changing colors of water lilies, neverwets, floating hearts, the pickerel weed, and the dainty bladderwort. And early-day explorer William Bartram wrote of seeing "isles of floating fields...decorated with amphibious plants."

The great swamp remains a significant part of America's heritage. Yet, it was almost lost when attempts were made to drain its waters in an effort to create farmland, when the logging industry came in to axe its cypress trees and take them from Billy's Island. But Georgians fought back, and the swamp was saved, now protected as a National Wildlife Refuge.

At the Okefenokee Swamp Park, a Serpentarium features an interpretive exhibit of reptiles, and a Wildlife Observatory looks at native bears in their natural environment. The Swamp Creation Center traces the history of the trembling earth, and The Living Swamp Center spotlights the flora and fauna from a live deer observatory. Boat tours follow winding water trails, and wilderness walkways lead back into the hidden recesses of a beautiful, primeval land that remains just as it was back when the dawn of America really began.

The Okefenokee has become America's greatest natural botanical garden. (Photo: Jimmy Walker)

26

PRESIDENTIAL PATHWAYS

His eyes were tired, and he hadn't farmed in years, but he remembered the rough years, the depression years, plowing ground where too many cotton crops had already ruined the Pine Mountain soil.

"We didn't have hardly nobody to help us back in those days," he said, and then a smile touched his face. "That's when FDR came along. Many an afternoon the President would drive right up in my yard, and we would talk for hours. He spent a lot of time talkin' to just about ever'body 'round here. I sometimes think that old FDR started all of those programs to help the workin' man get by simply because he cared about what was happenin' to his Georgia neighbors."

The peace of the National Cemetery at Andersonville belies the heartbreak, the tragedy of the War Between the States.

3.

$\mathcal{I}$t is sacred ground, back among the rolling hills, thick with piny woods, out across peanut fields where Presidents have left their footprints planted deep in rich Georgia soil.

Jimmy Carter is back in Plains, farming, as he has for a lifetime, with people who knew him, who believed in him as a friend and neighbor long before they witnessed his election as thirty-ninth chief executive of the United States.

His birthplace is there. So is his home. The warehouses in Plains stock his peanuts. And the little white depot once served as his campaign headquarters when he first said softly, "My name is Jimmy Carter, and I want to be your President."

No one gave him a chance.

But Georgia has had a long history of breeding proud, ambitious, and determined men who knew what they wanted and were willing to work hard and fight harder to get it.

The depot now houses memorabilia and exhibits from Carter's campaign and his Presidential years.

$\mathcal{O}$n a sunshiny day back in 1931, Franklin Delano Roosevelt was taking a horseback ride with a friend in the deep woods of Pine Mountain. There was no road. The trail was barely wide enough for a horse to travel. But the nature-loving man who was to become President knew where he was going.

Seven years earlier he had come to the peaceful area and found that swimming in the waters of Warm Springs had greatly improved his crippled condition. In 1926, Roosevelt acquired the springs, an old hotel, several

31

cottages, and 1,200 acres of land, even establishing the Georgia Warm Springs Foundation to aid others stricken with poliomyelitis.

It was a good land, he thought. It was where he belonged.

On that day, Franklin Roosevelt paused in the middle of a quiet pine forest, saying that he had always wanted a place to come home to in Georgia. Now at last he had found it.

The cottage he built there is simple, unpretentious, yet impressive, and it has become an internationally-known shrine to the President's memory. He once said he loved this plain Little White House more than any home he had ever had.

In the living room, the feldstone fireplace is as it was on April 12, 1945, the day he died. It even holds the same partly-burned logs. Beside the fireplace is the brown leather chair where Roosevelt sat, while Madame Elizabeth Shoumatoff was painting his picture, when the fatal stroke came. The unfinished portrait stands near where she had been working. It is a tragic moment, captured and frozen in time.

At Fort Benning's National Infantry Museum in Columbus, there are more Presidential mementos, including documents signed by most of the nation's chief executives, as well as gifts presented to them from international heads of state. And President William McKinley's bookcases can be found among the collections in The Veranda, one of the two bed and breakfast facilities in Senoia. The other is the Victorian Culpepper House, furnished in period furniture and collectibles.

The grand life of early Georgia is portrayed in its grand homes: Bellevue, the 1853 Greek Revival house in LaGrange that served as home for the famous statesman, Benjamin Hill, and Montezuma's House on Literary Hill, a Neo-Classical home with period furnishings. And historic driving tours lead past the gracious old homes of Columbus, Newnan, and Vienna.

Westville, near Lumpkin, is an authentic pioneer village, a tribute to those who first trampled across Georgia soil. It is a place where no clocks run, where time is measured by a boundary earmarked 1850. In reality, Westville has been reconstructed from the remnants of a dozen different Georgia communities, preserving the crafts of a tanner, brickmaker, candlemaker, shingle maker, blacksmith, potter, printer, ginner, and sawyer, all practiced in early-day rural hamlets.

A sadness enshrouds the Andersonville National Historic site, a Southern prison where more than 12,900 Union soldiers died. A restored Confederate Village includes a log church, pioneer farm, and quarters for officers at the prison. And the Drummer Boy Civil War Museum contains original uniforms, guns, swords, and battle flags from the terrible conflict.

It marks a heart-broken time, in a land where Presidents have walked, that is unforgotten, never to be forgotten.

The warmth of a President who found a home in Georgia is mirrored in Franklin D. Roosevelt's Little White House.

33

A Showcase of Beauty, of Nature in Full Bloom

Cason Callaway was a visionary.

He stood upon the highlands of the Georgia Piedmont, looked at the rolling, timbered land around him, and saw that it was good. And Cason Callaway immediately began to conceive of ways to make it better. He had long believed that the woods were made for the hunters of dreams...that gardens were born before gardeners...that even nature could sometimes use a helping hand. He gave it his own.

Cason Callaway planted his solitary dream in the ancient Piedmont soil, and, in time, it became the gardens that bear his name, nestled quietly alongside the gentle foothills of Pine Mountain. He brought a rich, vibrant color back to the hidden recesses of the forest again, blending azaleas and rhododendrons, hollies and dogwood, roses and wildflowers together upon 2,500 acres, where cotton had sapped the ground and erosion had cut unforgiving scars across farmlands, both abandoned and abused. The gardens would be Callaway's gift to mankind because, he once said, "Every child ought to see something beautiful before he is six years old, something he will remember all of his life."

He took the land as it was and nourished it, bringing life and beauty back to the surrounding countryside, weaving thousands of new flowers into those patches of native flora that clung valiantly to the piny wood hillsides.

And Callaway told his son, Bo, "We don't want to just build the finest garden seen on earth since Adam was a boy. What we want to do is build the prettiest garden that will ever be seen on earth 'til Gabriel blows his horn."

Callaway Gardens has become, as its founder hoped it would, a place to rejuvenate both the mind and the body, a showcase of beauty, of nature in full bloom, a refuge in an uncrowded woodland of oak and hickory and tulip poplar.

Cason Callaway had sensed and understood the need to build a special kind of place upon the Piedmont of Georgia. He once said, "If a man wanted to take his kids swimming, all that was available to him was a muddy frog pond. If he wanted to take his family on a picnic, the best place he could find was a cut-over forest of pine stumps."

He reasoned: "Rich men can always find a place of beauty to go, but it's the factory worker or salesman—everyman—who, with but limited funds, needs a place to go with his family for a happy quiet stay in beautiful surroundings."

They would forever find it at Callaway Gardens.

It is now recognized as one of the nation's top family resorts with a wide range of programs that appeal to every age. Callaway Gardens is indeed more than merely a home for azaleas and dogwoods. Down on the sandy beach of Robin Lake, there is miniature golf, paddleboats, canoes, and rides on either a riverboat or a train. During the summer months, the lake throbs with the high-

The beauty of Callaway Gardens is reflected in its woodland lakes.

jumping, acrobatic excitement of a daily Water Ski Spectacular. And in May, the nation's most respected, most revered daredevils on skis compete for world records in slalom, jumping, and tricks at the famed Masters Water Ski Tournament.

Back among the trees, in a setting landscaped by the beauty, the wilds, of nature itself, are 17 lighted tennis courts, supervised by a team of Callaway professionals who conduct classes, as well as give private lessons. In fact, *Tennis Magazine* has recognized Callaway Gardens as one of the fifty top tennis resorts in the United States.

There are thirteen lakes scattered throughout the 2,500 acres, spreading like mirrors back into the frontyard of the mountains, reflecting abstractly the giant trees that cast their shadowed images across wind-rippled water. Coots paddle playfully into the shelter of the coves, and mallards drift lazily like feathered buoys back amidst the pine needles that have fallen gently onto a tranquil surface. The silence is broken only by the whisper of the winds that flutter through the woodlands, by the sound of a lone angler's top-water bait as it splashes toward the shoreline. Fishing and boating are permitted on Mountain Creek Lake, stocked with bass and bream. The remaining dozen lakes have been saved to reflect the peace and serenity of a gentle forest.

Bicycle trails wind casually through the edge of the gardens. Year around, sportsmen can shoot trap or skeet. And during season, they can track down deer and quail on Callaway hunting preserves.

G. Harold Northrop, president and CEO of Callaway Gardens, points out, "What we try to do is give people a serene place with educational and inspirational qualities, plus all the recreational facilities. We want to give people a feeling of being close to the earth. After they have visited Callaway Gardens, we want people to take home with them consolation for the heart, nourishment for the soul, and inspiration for the mind."

Many find everything that they are searching for at the resort's tempting, intriguing sixty-three holes of golf on four championship quality courses.

Golf certainly gives them that feeling of being closer to the earth for awhile.

When the sport was introduced into the valley of the pines, those first nine fairways were carved into the forest with one thought in mind: "To make it extremely difficult for an amateur duffer to lose a ball."

Times have changed.

So has the challenge of golf at Callaway Gardens.

But one thing remains constant. It has always been the Gardens' philosophy that whenever a golfer made the mistake of lifting his head on a shot, he or she should be able to see something beautiful. So the lakes and the fairways are bordered with woodland plants and shrubs and magnolia trees—a fringe of floral lace in the foreground of the mountains.

Four championship courses provide 63 intriguing holes of golf.

Tommy Aaron, the 1973 champion of the prestigious Masters Golf Tournament, once explained: "The Mountain View course is more to the taste of the tournament player or the fellow who is looking for a challenge. You can play the championship tees there and stretch it out to 7,040 yards or play the reds and bring it down to the club player distance of 6,605 yards. From the ladies' tees, it's still 5,834 yards.

"Lake View is the oldest, a sporty kind of course that appeals to the vacation player. He's the type of golfer who likes to go home and tell his friends about a good score. He can score better on Lake View.

"The most scenic hole, the fifth hole, furnishes one of the most familiar and traditional golfing scenes in America. It is a 150-yard hole that crosses a lake. And it's all carry over water, playing toward that picturesque old clubhouse."

The summer recreation program, according to Ted Robison, executive vice president and managing director, is the reason that Callaway Gardens has become such a popular place for so many families for so many years. Talented student members of the Florida State University Flying Circus perform eight incredible shows a week beneath the Big Top alongside Robin Lake. But most of their time is spent supervising a varied schedule of activities for children at the Gardens.

As Robison explains, "On a typical Tuesday morning at 9:30, a three-year-old might be on a riverboat ride down on Robin Lake. A ten-year-old might be in the middle of a well supervised swimming class. A twelve-year-old might be learning to sail on Mountain Creek. A sixteen-year-old might be touring the vegetable garden. And their worry-free parents are off taking part in arts and crafts, aerobic dancing, a tennis class, golf lesson, or an ecology hike."

It is heard time and again from happy families: "This is the first vacation we've been on in several years when we weren't busy all the time with a small child."

Throughout the year at Callaway Gardens, there are workshops that demonstrate such activities as cooking with wild plants or arranging dried flowers. Seminars cover a variety of topics, including pruning, landscaping, and holiday decorating. There are interpretive walks along the Wildflower and Azalea Trails, through the Vegetable Garden, and beside the shoreline of Mountain Creek Lake, where birdwatchers in particular can keep an eye out for the 170 species of birds that come flocking to Callaway Gardens. Approximately 90 species have been catalogued in the wintertime alone, when wood ducks, canvasback, bufflehead and mallard ducks, Canada geese and pied billed grebes all migrate from northern lands, searching for warmer climes and finding them on the Garden lakes.

Fairways are bordered with woodland plants, flowers, and shrubs.

The accommodations and dining facilities at Callaway Gardens are nothing like home, nor were they meant to be.

The resort's Inn offers 345 rooms, many overlooking the Great Lawn, and all of them convenient to the dining rooms, lounges, tennis courts, and golf courses. For those seeking seclusion and privacy, however, the Mountain Creek Villas are hidden away beneath the pines, rustic, yet elegant, built of red cedar and native Georgia stone, designed to harmonize architecturally with the unspoiled beauty of the landscape. The Callaway Country Cottages, blending into the woodlands with cedar exteriors, all have two bedrooms, large dressing areas, fully equipped kitchens, woodburning fireplaces, screened porches, and decks. Nearby are an indoor/outdoor swimming pool, a children's playground, and restaurant.

Conference planners across the country are especially intrigued with the five-bedroom Executive Lodge which offers an exclusive environment for meetings and special entertaining. It has living and dining rooms, terraces and a game room with a bar, as well as a private swimming pool and tennis court. There are even cook, maid, and butler services available. In addition, three Roof Garden suites, located on the top floor of the resort's Inn, are elegantly furnished, and each contains a wet bar and terrace. The Roof Garden Boardroom is a superb meeting room, with a reception area and wet bar.

Dining at Callaway Gardens has always been a memorable experience, sometimes casual, sometimes sophisticated.

The Georgia Room at the Callaway Gardens Inn is wrapped in the aura and atmosphere of the early days down South, where dark woods and fine China glow in candlelight, and soft piano music sets a refined and romantic mood. It's the place for a roast rack of lamb with mint sauce, maybe quail with wild rice, or even Steak Diane.

The Gardens Restaurant, once the old clubhouse that overlooks the Lake View golf course, has a definite English country feel to it, with polished hardwood floors, exposed beams, and a huge, native flagstone fireplace. While the Musicana Singers are entertaining, the kitchen is turning out such down-home delicacies as pan-fried trout, aged steaks, shrimp, and Christine's own specially-flavored barbecued ribs.

Below the Gardens, the Veranda Restaurant serves dishes from around the world. It is decorated in romantic peach pastels and inlaid woods, and its French doors open onto a flagstone patio that looks out over the golf course.

The Plantation Room, at the Inn, offers such regional foods as Southern fried chicken. But it is legendary for its old-fashioned, unforgettable breakfast spread. So is the Country Kitchen Restaurant, located in back of the Country Store, as authentic and deeply Southern as the Speckled Heart Grits, muscadine preserves, and thick slabs of Georgia-cured bacon and ham that the cooks pile on a plate.

For light lunches, there is the Vineyard Green, an indoor garden with

40

robust hanging plants that surround an immense ficus tree. For quicker lunches—specialty sandwiches and jumbo hamburgers—The Flower Mill is unbeatable, and it even brings back the look, the feel, the taste of a dairy bar and fountain straight out of the rock 'n' roll era of the fifties.

At night, a live band entertains in the Vineyard Green, while the English library setting of the Patio bar appeals more to those who simply want a drink, do a little reading, or participate in a quiet game of backgammon or chess.

It was on a ridge near Blue Springs in 1930 when Cason Callaway stumbled upon a flowering shrub whose red-orange blooms resembled an azalea. He had never seen a flower quite like it before, and it would be a plant he could not forget.

Callaway carried a sprig home to his wife, Virginia, a knowledgeable horticulturist, a delicate woman who felt right at home in the woodlands. She identified the blossom as a prunifolia azalea, a sensitive flower that always bloomed long after other native azaleas had faded. It was a shrub so rare that it grew nowhere else on earth, only in a few scattered drifts within a hundred mile radius of Blue Springs.

Cason Callaway was a Georgia industrialist who had built his empire with textile mills. And he loved the land that was his home. For so long he had watched Virginia tending to wild plants—no matter how small or ragged—as they walked through the forest together. And he sought to share her appreciation of nature. Callaway made up his mind quickly to do what he could to preserve and protect the last dwindling and natural refuge of the prunifolia azalea. That meant acquiring land. So Cason Callaway began buying up large chunks of acreage around Blue Springs. For a time, it was merely a hideaway for him and Virginia. It would not stay that way forever.

He employed a man to wander the forestland and seek out the rare azalea and collect its seeds. His goal was to grow enough of them—beautiful and wild—so they would never be lost to the ages. The seeds—20,000 of them—were gathered, tenderly germinated, and the seedlings planted beside Blue Springs. Five years later they bloomed. And one day, they would form the nucleus of an eden called Callaway Gardens.

For two decades, Callaway was content to be a gentleman farmer, seeking new ways to cultivate the lowlands and make them fertile again. He planted muscadines, blueberries, and oats as alternatives to cotton. He slowly began to stabilize much of his eroded land with pines, even persuading the Better Farm program to implement his ideas on soil restoration.

Then he sought to beautify the land.

When Virginia requested a large magnolia tree for her birthday, he bought her 5,000 small ones as well. He became a gardener even while he was only dreaming of a garden.

In 1953, Callaway brought in Fred Galle as his director of horticulture to transform the gullies and hillsides. Galle had one responsibility: to make the gardens grow naturally, blending imported and native vegetation together so the new would look comfortably at home with the old. Galle said, "We hoped to do in twenty years what it would normally take nature, working alone, two centuries to accomplish."

And that was what they did. They focused on native material, from dogwoods to mountain laurel to native azaleas. They preserved plants, wildflowers, and trees in their natural setting. For the next fifteen years, Galle annually brought in 10,000 permanent trees and shrubs, and he christened the slopes with 700 different species and varieties of azaleas, making their collection one of the largest in the country.

When Callaway Gardens finally opened in May of 1952, two decades of hard work had already been invested in the land. But Cason Callaway saw his vision become a reality.

A scenic drive winds past Meadowlark Gardens, the world's largest display of holly, where English, American, Japanese, and Chinese hollies grow amidst camelias, winter tea olives, daffodils, and Oriental wildflowers. The Rhododendron Trail is aflame April and May with seventy-five different species. Laurel Springs is virtually undisturbed, providing a glimpse of a true Southern Appalachian forest. Seasonally, the dark woods are alive with the crested iris, dogwood, black-eyed Susan, the rare fringed pink, rose, and Confederate daisy.

An old log cabin is a reminder of life the way it was. The beautiful Ida Cason Callaway Memorial Chapel, a small sanctuary of English Gothic, gives inspiration for life. And the color of life never ceases to bloom on the woodland floor.

The magnificent, five million dollar, five-acre Sibley Center, according to Dr. Bill Barrick, director of gardens, is not a traditional greenhouse, even though it is under glass. He wants gardens to be an intimate part of everyone's life, both indoor and out, so footpaths lead behind a waterfall and on past flowers that are forever changing with the seasons. The center was named for John A. Sibley, who, like Callaway, fought for the land he called "God's most precious gift."

The nation's first butterfly center, a gift of Mrs. Deen Day Smith, has been patterned after similar conservatories in England and Scotland. It is dramatic. It is breathtaking. Butterflies from the world's tropics, called flying flowers, quietly carry out their metamorphosis and life span among the flora. To witness it, Hal Northrop says, is an "aesthetical and educational experience unlike any other in the country."

Cason Callaway once had a vision. The vision continues.

Callaway Gardens provides nourishment for both the body and the mind.

A Timeless
Reflection of Victorian Grace

In 1828, the governor of Georgia demanded that a fort be built to guard his people against Indian attack, and log posts were promptly hammered into the ground alongside the banks of the Chattahoochee River. Captain Basil Hall of the British navy reported: "The new city was to commence at the lower end of a long series of falls, or more properly speaking rapids, over which this great river dashes in a very picturesque manner. The perpendicular falls being about 200 feet, an immense power for turning mills is placed at the disposal of the inhabitants of the future city."

He was almost a prophet. The new and future city became Columbus. In time, the mills did come to harness the rapids. And to its shoreline ventured culture, then war, all reflected in the Victorian grace and elegance that is locked within the architectural spirit of Columbus.

Columbus, these days, situated where five major road systems intersect, likes to refer to itself as a city on the move at the center of the sunbelt South. After all, it is the state's second largest city with more than 2,000 quality hotel and motel rooms. And it remains a bustling industrial leader because national and international companies appreciate the superb quality of life in the area. Yet, Columbus keeps a firm grip on its legacy. Even the Columbus Iron Works, which manufactured the first commercial ice machine, as well as cannons and gunboats during the War Between the States, has been rebirthed as the city's convention and trade center.

Throughout Columbus have blown the winds of war. On exhibit at the Confederate Naval Museum are the remains of two Southern warships, the ironclad ram *Jackson* and the gunboat *Chattahoochee*, both rescued from their watery graves. The National Infantry Museum at Fort Benning displays more than 60,000 items, including 2,600 firearms, some dating back to the Revolutionary War, as it proudly traces two centuries of service by America's fighting men. The historic past of the region can be discovered in the Columbus Museum, the state's second largest. The museum also offers a youth-oriented gallery, as well as fine and decorative art galleries. The Springer, Opera House, the State Theatre of Georgia, also plays an active and vital role in the cultural life of Columbus.

Columbus, its scenic riverside now a promenade of gardens and gazebos, has long been recognized for its beautiful and memorable nineteenth-century homes. Several are open for daily tours by the Historic Columbus Foundation, including its headquarters, an 1870 Italianate townhouse. The Woodruff Farm House has a museum/gift shop. A log cabin typifies the kind of home a trader had before the settlement of Columbus. The Walker-Peters-Langdon House is an 1828 Federal cottage, believed to be the oldest house in town. And the Pemberton House was originally the home of Dr. John Smith Pemberton, who concocted the formula for Coca-Cola.

Columbus has long been known as a city of fountains.

A Remembrance of Times Past

Jt was a good land, a peaceful land, down among the thick pine forests where the Powers family all nailed their hopes, their dreams, their future onto a patch of rich Georgia soil. They cleared away the woodlands, shoulder to shoulder with the Creek Indians of Chief William McIntosh, and plowed new ground as the eighteenth century dimmed. The world around them seemed so untamed, so distant from any remnant of civilization.

After a time, a curious loneliness fell upon the land, as the Creeks abandoned their homesteads and were marched away down a grief-stricken Trail of Tears, headed West, leaving sacred ground that would never belong to their people again.

By 1870, John Powers became the fourth generation of his family to farm the land alongside the Coweta Trail. He was stubborn and defiant and self-sufficient. What he had, John Powers made with his own hands. What he couldn't make, he did without. It wasn't hardship. It was life.

On Labor Day weekend, the Powers' Crossroads Country Fair and Art Festival pays tribute to the craftmanship and traditions of those early-day settlers who in time shaped Georgia in their own image. A special selection committee chooses 300 remarkably talented artisans from throughout the United States and Canada. Their unique creations showcase the best crafts and fine art in all media that the nation has to offer.

The old-fashioned country fair was established on his ancestral acres by Tom Powers, a Georgia artist who sought to preserve the flavor of another era. Presently operated by the non-profit Coweta Festivals, Inc., it is located on the historic 1795 Powers Plantation, ten miles southwest of Newnan on Georgia Highway 34. The fair, rated as one of the top 100 events in North America, has been repeatedly listed as one of the top twenty events in the nine Southeastern states region.

It is a faded piece of history restored as exhibitors gather beneath massive oaks. Nearby, old fashioned children's activities are revived and supervised by adults at the Twin Oaks Junction Children's Park. The original crossroads grist mill grinds corn meal and wheat flour. Syrup is cooked in copper vats at an old sorghum cane mill, powered by plodding, unhurried mules. A moonshine still produces white lightning, just as it did back during the days when backroads farmers realized that a bushel of corn was worth a lot more when distilled. The old country store, built from railroad box car lumber, is again stocked with turn-of-the-century wares. The store is surrounded by the Georgia Carriage Association's exhibit of vintage rolling stock, featuring carriages, hunting traps, surreys, wagons, and even a rare horsedrawn hay bailer.

There is the lonesome wail of a bluegrass fiddle, the rhythm of mountain clog dancers, the patriotic fervor of a military band, the aroma of down-home cooking, heavy on the barbecue sauce. The Powers' Crossroads Fair has the definite flavor of a historic time that was but will never be again.

Craftsmen and artists both demonstra their work with the professionalism Don McWhirter.

NORTHEAST GEORGIA MOUNTAINS

The prospector of the 1980s was waist deep in muddy water, and there was a twinkle buried deep within his graying eyes. The first time he had ever mined the waters of Etowah Creek, he had come up with five and a half ounces of gold, and the old prospector had not been the same since.

He said, ''There just ain't nothing better in the world than looking for gold all day, then flopping down on a creek bank at night. You make a fire, wrap a mountain trout in tinfoil, and throw it in the ashes. You sleep awhile. Get up. And you wait for daylight to roll around. You never know what morning's gonna give you. Sometimes it's gold.''

*The high country is captured in the
colorful splendor of a changing season.*

4.

The Indians believed in an unseen mystical power that trekked a wild, forbidden country, up where the earth reached high to touch the clouds. They whispered softly of Sal-un-yi, whose spirit stood sentinel over the mountains, who placed his blessing upon hallowed, blood-stained ground and dared mankind to find the wealth that he had left scattered in the dark hollows of the woodlands. Many have searched for it.

And in those small, sparkling, cold-water streams that flow out of the mountains around Blairsville, they have found small nuggets of gold, ruby chips, brown sapphires, and stones of tiger's eye. The land has indeed been blessed.

Dahlonega crowns the Northeast Georgia hills with the grace and reverence that has always been reserved for the rich. And Dahlonega knows all about being rich. On a fateful day in 1828, old Ben Parks kicked over a rock while deer hunting and discovered that it was streaked with veins of gold. Thus began the first gold rush in America. It would be another twenty-one years before the famed forty-niners headed west for California and a little creek by Sutter's Mill.

The amount of gold taken from those Dahlonega hills was staggering. The U.S. Government even built a mint there to turn raw flakes into money. And during the next decade, that mint fashioned 1,378,871 coins worth more than $6.1 million.

There's still gold in the mountains. The area's history is on display at the Dahlonega Gold Museum in the old country courthouse. And Crisson's Gold Mine makes it easy to pan for flakes. A wizened prospector says, "Put the pan

51

underwater and work the dirt with your hands like you were working up dough. Take out all the little rocks you find, but don't ever remove any of that black sand. That's where the gold is. Keep shaking it, and the gold will settle to the bottom."

Overlooking the land of hidden wealth is Brasstown Bald, the highest mountain in Georgia. And at the summit, 4,784 feet above sea level, there rises an imposing structure that some say resembles a rocket ready for launching. Others believe that it looks more like a flying saucer that has just landed. Actually, it is a fire lookout tower with a visitor's center and observation deck that looks out across four states.

Looming in the near distance are Slaughter and Blood Mountains, named for battles fought there between Creeks and Cherokee. The old Cherokee War Trail slips out of the high country and down into Vogel State Park, a land between the Alpine village of Helen and Blairsville that still clings to Indian lore. Lake Trahlyta was even named for a Cherokee princess. As long as she drank from the waters of the spring beside her home, Trahlyta remained young and beautiful. But, alas, she fell in love with the warrior of another tribe and fled with him into the forest. When she left the spring water, she soon became old and haggard, and she died. Trahlyta lies buried at Stone Pile Gap, and everyone who passes her grave, legend says, must gently place another rock upon the cairn.

The mountain range surrounds rural Northeast Georgia like a timbered wall. Covered bridges, relics from another time, cross the roadways outside of Carnesville and Helen. Shelves at the Old Sautee Store, also near Helen, are stacked with the kind of merchandise that pioneers might have found there in the 1800s. And Dillard's Hambridge Center features such crafts as handweaving and pottery.

The Appalachian Trail begins atop Springer Mountain, in the Chattahoochee National Forest, and winds northward for two thousand miles to Maine. Nearby, Amicalola Falls, the tallest of Georgia's tumbling waters, drops in slender, ribbon-like threads for 729 feet. Toccoa was named for a Cherokee word meaning *beautiful*, and its Tocca Falls is, cascading like a veil of lace for 186 feet into a quiet little valley. That makes it twenty feet higher than Niagara Falls. The gorge at Tallulah Falls is reported to be the oldest in Eastern North America, a rugged canyon that ranges in depth from 200 to 1,200 feet. And the Chatooga is a vicious, yet pristine, wild-water river that defies rafts, canoes, and kayaks.

It is a land where the earth does touch the clouds, and its blessings remain unforgotten, never to be forgotten.

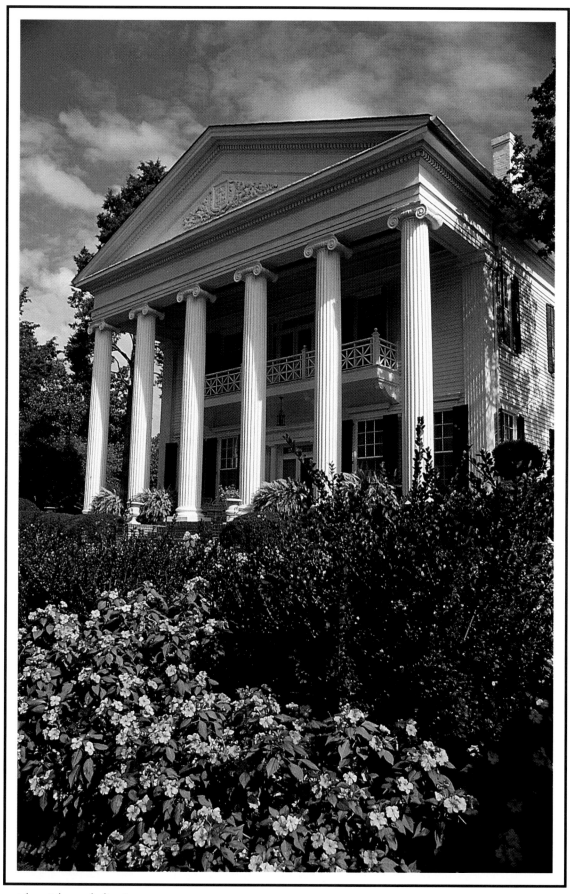

Oak Hill rises with pride and dignity above the campus of Berry College in Rome.

53

A Pioneering Spirit Forges Ahead

For so long, the lyrically rugged countryside that became Gwinnett County lay in the shadows of great cathedral forests, interlaced with the unspoiled beauty of unhurried and hidden waterways. It sheltered the Creek and the Cherokee, and only occasionally could the smoke from a homesteader's cabin be seen curling above the timber line. It was a quiet land, a good land, untrammaled and at peace with itself.

By 1818, both tribes had ceded their holdings to the U.S. Government, and within days the woodlands began to echo the sounds of pioneer farmers who were building homes, then villages from hand-hewn logs. The new county was named for Button Gwinnett, a signer of the Declaration of Independence who had helped frame most of Georgia's constitution.

Farmsteads, then great plantations were carved out of the fertile soil, their fields blanketed with cotton, grain, and vegetables. Gwinnett kept beckoning, and few could resist its temptation. Only four decades ago, the county housed less than 20,000. But now, more than 300,000 call it home, and Gwinnett was recognized each year from 1983 to 1987 as the fastest growing county in the nation. More and more, a land that was once dependent solely on the good earth for survival, now reflects the dynamic, high-tech face of the New South. Wedged between Lake Lanier and Stone Mountain, it is proud and affluent, a suburban cornerstone of Atlanta where fine, luxury accommodations can still be found at reasonable prices. New industry is a bold sculpture on the skyline. Road Atlanta throbs with the rhythm of racing cars and motorcycles.

Yet, the smaller communities of Gwinnett County have been reluctant to let go of the past. They are quaint reminders of those days when cotton plantations relied upon the railroads, and hamlets grew up around harness and saddle factories. Grand victorian homes, architectural testaments to the glory days of the 1890s, have been preserved and restored in both Norcross and Buford. The stoic, imposing courthouse of Lawrenceville overlooks the old town square just as it has for more than a century, a time-worn monument to the county's rich heritage.

Old Town Lilburn is a renovated collection of shops on its original Main Street, selling antiques, dolls, miniatures, and crafts, all spotlighted each year during the Lilburn Daze Arts Festival. Dacula is slow paced, a realistic glimpse of the old South. Duluth headlines an autumn festival of singing and dancing, arts and crafts to show off its proud past, as do Norcross, Sugar Hill, Suwanee, Grayson, and Snellville, whose motto is "Everybody is somebody." Lawrenceville's Summer Days fills the sky with hot air balloon races, and its fall event focuses on World War II vintage airplanes and stunt flying. Nearby, Tribble Mill is being developed into a 640-acre park with public beaches, fishing, boating, and camping. And out of the Yellow River Game Ranch, bear, mountain lions, and buffalo roam, and the land is as it was in the beginning.

The Courthouse is a time-worn monument, overlooking the Lawrenceville square.

Chateau Elan Winery

In the Image of
16th Century France

In Dublin, Ireland, on that chilly February day in 1988, all eyes were focused with uncertainty and expectation on an unusual three-case lot of Fume Blanc, Chardonnay, and Cuvee Charlemagne Chardonnay from, of all places, the mountains of North Georgia. The finest wines world wide had been chosen for a special auction on the Irish isle, and among them was a selection of Chateau Elan, imported from the faraway vineyards of Braselton, Georgia. In fact, Chateau Elan had the rare distinction of being the only wine there from the United States. Many wondered if it would be accepted internationally. The answer came quickly enough.

The Chateau Elan wines sold for one thousand dollars. But that should not have been too surprising. After all, in only two years, the wines had been awarded sixty-three medals in national competition, quite a feat for a small winery tucked away in mountains where commercial vineyards were a novelty.

Chateau Elan Ltd. owns one thousand acres in Barrow, Jackson, and Gwinnett Counties, about thirty miles north of Atlanta. Chardonnay, Riesling, Cabernet Sauvignon, Sauvignon Blanc, Chambourcin, and Seyval Blanc are currently being grown upon one hundred rolling acres. And the company's state of the art winery is presently bottling 25,000 cases a year. Chateau Elan's specialty, however, is subtle, elegant, fruity wines that do not need to be aged for years before being enjoyed.

When Donald E. Panoz established the U.S. branch of his Irish-based Elan pharmaceutical company in Gainesville, he wanted to further develop the striking land around him. An inveterate wine lover, Panoz decided to create a winery and recreation center, even though, traditionally, Georgia had never been known as a wine state. He pointed out, "I like the challenge of doing something nobody else is doing. Anybody can produce wine in California. I simply wanted to know why it couldn't be done in Georgia as well. The climate is perfect for growing grapes, and I am firmly convinced that a blend of tradition and technology could produce first class wines."

Panoz brought the remarkable talents of Jean Courtois to Georgia as his resident wine maker. Courtois is a descendant from many generations of renown wine makers, and his family owns a vineyard near the famed Chateauneuf-du-Pape district of France. By 1984, Chatau Elan was releasing its first wines and already receiving national acclaim.

The exterior of Chateau Elan Visitors Center captures the essence of a large French country house, built during the 16th century Renaissance Period. The character of a French street is reflected inside, where you find a history of wine exhibit, a French bistro restaurant, and a boutique. And free winery tours and tastings are offered every day.

For Donald Panoz, it was all a gamble. But he knew it could be done, and he did it.

*Chateau Elan blends the features
four famous 16th century Frenc
chateaux.*

56

Lake Lanier Islands

A Peaceable Kingdom in the Hills

Until the late fifties, only timbered hills rose up to crown the rugged landscape north of Atlanta, creased by the tumbling waters of the Chattahoochee and Chestatee Rivers. Mostly, it was an unsettled land, pristine and rural, far off-the-beaten path and content to stay that way.

In 1957, however, the Army Corps of Engineers dammed up those free-flowing, tumbling waters and created Lake Lanier, and the timbered hills that clustered north of Atlanta would never be a secret again. The water filled isolated valleys that ambled through five counties, and the forested hilltops emerged as islands that have more than 500 miles of shoreline. With fourteen million visitors a year, Lake Lanier is by far the most heavily used of all impoundments in the country.

It has all the appearances of a perfect bass lake. Some fishermen search the red clay shorelines for Kentucky spotted bass with worms and spinners. Other anglers constantly battle white bass, weighing only an average of three pounds each, but all fight. And, during the winter, the big freshwater striped bass—many weighing as much as forty pounds—lie in waiting.

Yet, the awesome depths of Lake Lanier—some holes drop as far below the surface as 160 feet—even make it possible for cold-water fish to survive. Rainbow trout congregate in deep pools beside Buford Dam, and Walleyes, native to Northern lakes, hug the bottom of Lanier's south end. To find them all is a challenge. To catch them is an art. But it is an art that many have mastered. A quarter of a million bass and 25,000 trout are taken out of Lake Lanier every year.

According to Roy Burson, executive director of the vast complex, Lake Lanier Islands is a 1,200 acre, 365-day festival of land and water. Comfortable two-bedroom cottages come with sundecks. A Conference Center overlooks the docks. And there is both recreational vehicle and tent camping at 314 peaceful, wooded, out-of-the-way sites, complete with charcoal grills, picnic tables, electrical and sewage hookups. Nearby are tennis courts, a swimming pool, and stables offering horseback rides that cut through miles of scenic, backcountry trails.

Lake Lanier Islands operates the largest fleet of inland rental craft in Georgia, with houseboats, group boats, pontoon boats, even versatile sport boats for fishing or sightseeing. Down on the sandy, white beach, stretching for almost three-fourths of a mile, are paddleboats and canoes, and sailboats reach out to catch a whisper of wind in the valley. Alongside the rippled sands, a water park looms as refreshing as it is exciting. The Breakers reigns as one of the Southeast's largest wavepools, much like an ocean without the saltwater. And the Chattahoochee Rapids inner tube slide is one of four slides that has more twists and turns than a giant pretzel. They are, some say, the wildest things anyone can do in a bathing suit.

For everyone, Lake Lanier and its timbered islands have become a private and a peaceable kingdom.

The wave pool is much like an ocean without saltwater.

The Dillard House

An Old-Fashioned Taste
of Country Hospitality

Almost two centuries ago, the brothers Dillard, James and John, trekked in to the extreme northeast mountains of Georgia and were convinced that they had found God's country. If not, it was close enough, and the Dillards, generation after generation, have never found any reason to search for any better or more beautiful land to call home.

John and James Dillard did leave for awhile, but that was back during the French and Indian War, then later during the Revolutionary War. But as soon as the last shots were fired, peace had been restored, and independence finally won, the brothers packed up and headed back to the Georgia mountains and to their beloved valley again.

They looked at those peaks which rose up above them, liked what they saw, and bought up all the land that lay between them, paying the Indians a muzzle loading rifle, a jug of apple brandy, and three dollars in hard-earned cash.

For generations, the Dillards made their living off the land, and they were known far and wide for their old-fashion, down-home hospitality. No one hungry was ever turned away from their table at supper time.

Just before the turn of the century, a new circuit-riding preacher came to the village of Clayton. His room had not yet been finished, so Arthur and Carrie Dillard invited him to move in with them. He was only supposed to stay three weeks. But he liked Mama Dillard's cooking so well that he stayed for several years. It was then that the idea was conceived for the Dillard House Inn. It sits perched on a knoll, overlooking one of Georgia's most scenic Smoky Mountain valleys, and it is an outstanding example of an old-time country boarding house that has managed to keep up with the times.

Through the years, more than a million guests—including governors, generals, and movie stars—have sampled the inn's mountain cooking, always featuring fresh farm-grown vegetables; hams, sausages, and bacon, specially cured in the Dillard's own smokehouse; grits; and red-eye gravy, as well as jellies, jams, relish, fresh breads, and homemade desserts.

The Dillard House Inn today is a self-contained resort, catering to families who are looking for first class lodging facilities and the finest in mountain cooking. It offers a variety of activities, such as swimming, tennis, horseback riding, a farm animal zoo, and nightly entertainment in its pavillion. Only minutes away, among tumbling waterfalls, are streams where outdoorsmen can fish for trout, pan for rubies, or raft the churning white-water rapids of the Chatooga. The famed Appalachian Trail winds through the high country, and a hiking path leads to the top of Georgia's highest mountain.

The Dillard House may be hidden away near Clayton. But it's not hard to find, and the inn is certainly worth the time that it takes to get there.

The Dillard House has become a legend in the Georgia mountains.

The Highland
Glimpse of an Alpine Village

For a time, it did not seem as though Helen stood a ghost of a chance. The Indian mound builders came in 10,000 B.C., but they didn't stay forever. A logging camp died away when the great virgin forest was all harvested. Traces of gold dust almost created a genuine boom town. But, alas, richer deposits of gold were found elsewhere, so the few ramshackle buildings became a ghost town, always a ghost town, again. Helen could have faded away, but its people were too stubborn for that.

Helen today is a picturesque little Alpine village, simply located in the Nacoochee Valley instead of the Alps.

In the early 1970s, three residents, Jim Wilkins, Bob Fowler, and Pete Hodkinson, met for lunch one day and observed that while the surrounding mountains were quite dramatic, their town plainly was not. It was dull and ordinary at best.

They wondered if something could be done to make Helen, population 250, more attractive. Hodkinson went to see a friend, an artist, John Kollock, who had been stationed in the Bavarian Alps. Kollock had long believed the morning veil of mist in the valley and the chattering Chattahoochie would be perfect backdrops for an Alpine village.

He made a series of color sketches showing how Helen would look with a fresh facade, and the townspeople were impressed. They began transforming their drab little hamlet into an architectural glimpse of Bavaria, a story book village of gables, rocco towers, gingerbread balconies, and scalloped fascia boards. Wooden signs were hung from wrought iron standards. A vacant lot was even converted into a charming cobblestone alley, lined with Old World shops that offer imports from Germany, Austria, and Switzerland, as well as from other countries around the globe. Not far from a new outlet mall are candy stores, bake shops, leather shops, and all along Helen's streets are working crafts people such as a dulcimer maker, woodturners, glassblowers, and engravers who make their crystal sparkle like diamonds. And on the faces of the buildings, Kollock, Nina Deiss, and other artists created scenes depicting the history of the countryside in murals reminiscent of the "air paintings" found in Bavaria.

Window boxes are everywhere, planted with petunias, dahlias, and geraniums. On the hour, bells atop the tower of White Horse Plaza, fill the downtown with the sounds of music, echoing out toward the blue, misty mountains which hide the Appalachian trail, out where the graceful fairways of a world class 18-hole golf course cut through the valleys.

On the edge of town, the old Nora Mill still grinds grain the old fashioned way. And the Museum of the Hills recreates authentic mountain life around the turn of the century, first at a farm house, then down the mainstreet of a quaint country village. It looks a lot like Helen did, back before an artist came to touch it with the Bavarian strokes of his brush.

Entries in Helen's Hot Air Balloon Festival rise above the Alpine village.

NORTHWEST GEORGIA MOUNTAINS

On a cold December day in 1835, the frail, ashen-faced John Ridge stood in the capital of New Echota, high in the mountains of Georgia, and looked across the gathering of Cherokees who had come to decide the fate of their nation.

"I know we love the graves of our fathers," he said. "We can never forget these homes, I know, but an unbending, iron necessity tells us we must leave them. Any forcible effort to keep them will cost us our lands, our lives, and the lives of our children."

It was the saddest day the Cherokees had ever known.

The vista across Mount Yonah spills out beyond the blue haze of the Georgia highlands.

5.

The high, rugged mountain terrain of northwest Georgia is stained with blood and with tears. The brave gave their lives to conquet a land that could not be conquered. The brave wept when they were forced, at gunpoint, to turn their backs on the graves of their fathers and leave it.

The Indians came first to find a refuge, then a home, in the highland wilderness. Their ancient Etowah Mounds, near Cartersville, are the sacred reminders of a thriving center for political and religious life which spanned five centuries in the little river valley. A museum illustrates the history of the village, and clay ramps lead to the top of the mounds, where the temples of chieftains and priests once stood.

Their time on earth remains a mystery.

Neither can anyone explain a puzzling fortification that rises in ruin upon the mountains near Chatsworth. No trace, no record has ever been found of the men who piled those rocks together for protection against an unknown foe. It could have been the Indians, or Conquistadors searching for gold, maybe 12th century Welse adventurers, or even the strange "moon-eyed people," white tribesmen who once roamed the woodlands. Their time on earth, too, has been lost with the ages.

The Cherokees found peace where the earth was old, and they called themselves the real people, the principle people. They were savage, but never savages, and they built fine homes and lived a gracious and a civilized life in the fertile valleys of the Blue Ridge.

Near Calhoun is the reconstruction of New Echota, capital of the Cherokee Nation in 1825. It was here that a print shop published the first Cherokee alphabet, then a newspaper, and for the first time the tribe could actually read in its own language. A walking tour connects a museum, describing the nation's turbulent years; the print shop; the Supreme Court building; the original Worcester House; and Vann Tavern.

Throughout the highlands are proud architectural traces of the Cherokees. At Canton, the tribe's battleground lies sprawling amidst the Blue Ridge Mountains. The two-story log home of Chief John Ross can be found at Rossville. Chief John Ridge's house is now the Chieftain's Museum at Rome. And the Vann house, between Dalton and Chatsworth, is a prime example of Cherokee wealth and culture in the early 1800s.

Then gold was found. And greed uprooted the Indians, and guns shoved them ever westward. They left their tears, but never their dignity, on a long, torturous trail that led them far beyond the boundaries of their mountain homeland.

Civil war spilled blood across the backbone of Georgia.

At Big Shanty, Union spies stole a locomotive, hoping to burn bridges on the way to Chattanooga. But Confederate gave chase and ran them down, and seven raiders met the hangman.

Death stalked the steep slopes of Kennesaw Mountain, and Atlanta lay in seige beneath the pungent smoke of gunfire.

Yet, in the brush and briar thickets of Chickamauga were fought, often hand to hand, some of the most unforgiving and desperate battles of the War Between the States. Confederates lost 18,000 men, and, when the guns had at last been silenced, Union forces had suffered 16,000 casualties.

Northern troops were forced to retreat back to the high country of Chattanooga, waiting to fight, waiting to die another bloody day in the shadow of Lookout Mountain.

A Kansas officer remembered, "We advanced under a perfect shower of bullets, sometimes driving the enemy and in turn being driven by them, until we had fought over the ground over and over again, and almost half of our number lay dead and wounded." A Confederate general called the Chickamauga, the "River of Death." The battlefield, in 1895, was one of the first to be established as a national military park.

In the town of Chickamauga, the Gordon-Lee House, aglow in antebellum splendor, served as a Union hospital during the two bloodiest days of fighting. The Whitman-Anderson House in Ringgold served as General U. S. Grant's headquarters during the war. Sherman stayed at Oakleigh in Rome. And some rest forever in the little Confederate Cemetery of Calhoun.

Those were the days of blood and of tears that remain unforgotten, never to be forgotten.

The falls of a white-water stream churn through the wilderness high country.

A Delicate Blending
of the Old and the New

The untamed rapids of the Chattahoochee, the River of Painted Rocks, spill out of the high country, tumbling toward their ultimate meeting with the Gulf, sweeping majestically along carved rock palisades, through timbered gorges, and past clustered shoal outcropping where brook, rainbow, and brown trout are hiding away in deep, cool water.

Among the aging limbs of a climax hardwood forest scamper rabbits, squirrels, quail, muskrat, and beaver. Pottery and crudely-fashioned relics from a long-ago Mississippian culture have been dug from the dirt of Indian rock shelters. Remnants of a Union Army trench, surrounded by scattered rifle pits, can still be seen guarding, with their memories, the river's shoreline. The men of Sherman marched here and fought here and died here, beside the untamed rapids of the Chattahoochee.

The river has long been the lifeline of Cobb County, tucked away in the shadows of the North Georgia mountains. But it was the railroad that brought growth, then war, then a rebirth to a land that holds the graves of almost 15,000 fallen soldiers in its National and Confederate Cemeteries.

The development of Marietta, founded on Cherokee lands in 1834, really began with construction of the Western & Atlantic Railroad that ran between Atlanta and Chattanooga. And, in time, it became a thriving cultural resort as wealthy planters came to soak themselves in its therapeutic spring waters. Even today, the face of Marietta mirrors the good life of those days gone by. Its Welcome Center, with exhibits and a film presentation, is located in the old passenger depot of the A&W Railroad. Carriage rides rumble down the tree-lined streets of its two national register historic districts, past antebellum and Victorian homes that have been beautifully preserved, all capturing the sentiment of the Old South.

It is a city that prides itself on the restoration of its past. Yet, Marietta works hard and successfully to keep pace with the dynamic world of a changing and contemporary Georgia. Popular musicals and experimental dramas both are presented on stage of the community's sophisticated Theatre in the Square. Monthly art shows share space with touring exhibits at the Marietta/Cobb Fine Arts Center, housed near the square in an 1893 building. Jogging and hiking trails wind along the scenic Chattahoochee River National Recreation Area. Not far away, the 12,000-acre Lake Allatoona offers swimming, boating and fishing, and Lake Acworth boasts a 400-yard sandy beach. Tennis courts are scattered throughout Marietta's forested parks. Polo players clash in noble competition at the Atlanta Polo Grounds. And during the summer each year, golf's leading money winners on the PGA tour battle in the Atlanta Golf Classic, played across the beautiful Atlanta Country Club course in eastern Cobb County.

Six Flags Over Georgia remains as one of the nation's premier theme

Top: Rafts crowd the docile waters of the Chattahoochie. (Photo: © 1988 Joel Gilmore)
Bottom: White water splashes away the heat of a summer sun. (Photo: © Joel Gilmore)

parks, with musical revues and heart-throbbing thrill rides all linked to the romance, the excitement of the state's colorful history. And White Water is a 35-acre park with river raft rides, speed slides, and body flumes only minutes away from the steel-and-glass skyscrapers of downtown Atlanta. It is as tame as the Little Hooch, namesake of the Chattahoochee, gently flowing and beckoning to those who simply want to worship the sun atop an inner tube. And White Water is as wild as the Dragon's Tail, a triple-drop slide, or the Gulf Screamer, where white knuckles hang onto inner tubes that come flying down a pair of fiberglass flumes. The park's man-made Atlanta Ocean holds 750,000 gallons of water, generating four-foot coastal waves in the mountains.

Throughout Cobb County, there is a blending of the new with the old. Artists of the South Cobb Arts Alliance turn out their creations of sculpture, paintings, glass, and leather in small hideaway studios. But their work is found at the Sweetwater Arts Gallery in Mableton, showcased in the 1834 Mable Home. Antique stores and galleries cluster along the streets of Smyrna, Kennesaw and Vinings, upon the same ground that shook with the thunder and the ferocity of war.

Marietta's 1885 Kennesaw House Hotel, now a popular restaurant, is where Andrew's Raiders, a band of northern spies, met in 1862, the night before they stole the *General* and began the great locomotive chase through Georgia. Andrews had a simple but daring plan. He and his men would board the train as it halted in Marietta, take it during a breakfast stop in Big Shanty, then race madly northward, destroying the bridges on the way to Chattanooga. But he had not counted on the tenacity of the conductor, William A. Fuller.

Fuller and Jeff Cain, who had been at the throttle, ran after the *General* on foot. At Moon's Station, they grabbed a platform car. At McGuire's Curve, they jumped aboard a small locomotive. And at Adairsville, they finally took command of the *Texas*, running it full speed in reverse until they at last caught the fleeing band of Andrew's Raiders eighty-seven miles and eight hours on down the track. Andrews and seven of his men, declared spies, were captured and hanged.

For decades, the *General* sat abandoned and virtually forgotten. Then in 1967, Chattanooga Mayor Ralph Kelly and his officials captured the historic locomotive in their city's freight yard to prevent its return to Kennesaw and the Big Shanty Fair. It took another five years of courtroom battles between the State of Georgia and city of Chattanooga before the Supreme Court finally ruled that the L & N Railroad had the sole right to give the locomotive to anybody it pleased.

And the L & N let the *General* go home to a museum at Big Shanty Crossing in Kennesaw Station, from where it had been stolen in the first place.

Top: Glover Park is surrounded by the tranquility of Marietta Square. (Photo: © 1988 Betsy Harbison, Atlanta Stock Associates)
Bottom: The General *sits proudly in the Big Shanty Museum.* (Photo: © 1988 Flip Chalfant)

The Guns of War
Rocked Kennesaw Mountain

Abraham Lincoln, in 1864, was facing a year of decision. Many in the North had become weary of war and were searching for compromise, even if it meant allowing secession. In order to retain the Presidency, he desperately needed victories.

He needed Atlanta, the rail hub, the manufacturing center of the Confederacy.

But the barrier to Atlanta was General Joseph E. Johnston and 60,000 men, all dug into the slopes of Kennesaw Mountain.

Johnston waited while Union General William T. Sherman began marching three armies with 100,000 men southward from Chattanooga, praying that the difficult terrain of his highland fortress would make up for the disparity in numbers. He also had the weather on his side. For a month, the rains had come, turning the roadways into mud quagmires, completely stalling Sherman's advance. There were skirmishes and artillery duels. One battle took place across Kolb's farm, six miles away, but, in general, the weather seemed more unbearable than combat.

Sherman's armies became impatient. They wanted to fight.

At nine o'clock on the morning of June 27, the general granted their wish. Two major offenses were unleashed against Johnston's fortifications at Pigeon and Cheatham Hills. Both failed. It's said that even the Southern defenders shuddered at the carnage. When night came, the Federal toll ran almost three thousand. The Confederates had lost eight hundred men.

In July the rains stopped and the roads were hardening again. Sherman's march headed southwest, and Johnston dropped his force back toward Atlanta. At that time, a displeased Jefferson Davis relieved Johnston of his command, replacing him with General John B. Hood while the Confederates were engaged in battles at Peachtree Creek, Ezra Church, and Jonesboro.

The seige of Atlanta had begun. Lincoln would soon have the victories he needed, and his reelection was assured.

Today, Kennesaw Mountain, located two miles north of Marietta, is a 2900-acre National Battlefield Park. At its visitor center, a museum traces the history of the Atlanta campaign with particular emphasis on the fighting within the area.

A one-mile mountain road leads to the summit of Big Kennesaw Mountain and to a short trail that winds past exhibits and gun emplacements to a magnificant overlook of the rugged terrain that became Atlanta's last, futile hope.

About five miles away, also in the park, is Cheatham Hill, and a quarter-mile walk, past a trail of original Confederate earthworks, silent memorials to those tragic days, leads to the Illinois Monument. Kolb Farm has been restored, appearing much as it did during the war. An exhibit there helps recapture that June 22 scene when John B. Hood's Confederate Corps struck the Union position at the farm, then withdrew with heavy losses.

Hiking trails retrace the footsteps of the soldiers in battle, and all encompass some moderately steep climbing.

Top: Kennesaw Mountain is now a 2,900-acre battlefield park. (Photo: © 1988 Flip Chalfant)
Bottom: Memories of the past are conjured up at the Brumby Rocker Museum. (Photo: © 1988 Betsy Harbison, Atlanta Stock Associates)

A Day to Remember, The Thrill of a Lifetime

Atlanta's Six Flags Over Georgia, during the past two decades, has become the premiere theme park in the Southeast. Its thrill rides are awesome. Its entertainment is top notch and captivating. Its musical shows are designed to put a song in your heart and a dance in your step.

But then, Six Flags, since day one, has always maintained the same basic philosophy. That, President Spurgeon Richardson points out, "is to provide quality entertainment for all members of the family."

There is, as the old saying goes, something memorable for everyone. No one is left out or overlooked.

The Showcase Theatre, for example, traces musical history in its professional production of "Starstruck." There is a real old-fashioned, happy-go-lucky, foot-tapping revue, "Good Times, Good Music, Good Friends," in the Crystal Pistol, with all the trappings of a music hall that works hard and works successfully to capture the spirit and the aura of an earlier time, back in the days when Georgia was a little wilder and a lot more rowdy.

All the world may not be a stage. But all of Six Flags Over Georgia is.

The nationally-acclaimed David Blackburn, who produces the shows for Six Flags, takes a special pride in the talent, the care, and the quality that are diligently interwoven into the fast-paced musical revues. The park is never silent. Somewhere across those beautiful, well-landscaped, and well maintained 331 acres, there is always a show going on. And the sounds of music are never that far away.

Blackburn says, "These young people have such energy, such enthusiasm. Everytime anyone sees a presentation, it is like watching the show for the very first time."

For the children, Bugs Bunny[TM], Daffy Duck[TM], and the whole gang—Sylvester[TM], Wile E. Coyote[TM], and Foghorn Leghorn—get together for an uplifting presentation in the Looney Tunes Theatre. It's called "The Fun Factory Show," and, with music and magic, it promotes the simple, yet important, messages of friendship, courtesy, self-esteem, and the love for others. The characters wander throughout the park, appealing to the playful nature in everyone. Their role is a simple one. They make people laugh. Maybe that's the most important role of all.

And as soon as the sun goes down, Graffiti's innovative teen club lights up, throbbing with the rhythms of the latest dance music and video hits, giving young people a place and an opportunity to dance the night away.

In the distance, nostalgic lights glow on the intricate, handcarved, and historic Riverview Carousel, a bright and colorful survivor of Chicago's famed Riverview Amusement Park. And it beckons from a high, wooded knoll, showcasing more than seventy-five individually designed horses, carriages, and mythical figures, standing five abreast.

Talent and energy are generated from the shows at Six Flags.

Then comes the thrill. The pulse beats wildly. There are dry mouths and sweaty palms.

And screams.

Brightly-painted cars and trains are catapulted across tubular tracks. The world races past at what seems like breakneck and unthinkable speeds.

Then it's upside down.

Again.

At Six Flags Over Georgia, the search goes on for the ultimate coaster, one that defies gravity, takes your breath away, squeezes your knuckles white, and puts what is left of your heart in your throat. Or maybe the search has ended. Maybe there is no reason to look beyond the tracks of Z Force.

Z Force, new and riveting, sponsored by WAGA-TV5 in Atlanta, is a 1900-foot-long coaster with steep ascents that rise dramatically and fearfully to almost seventy-five feet above the ground. Then it comes sweeping down the tracks, bolting through a series of vertical drops and lightning corkscrew dives, changing speeds with every twist and turn.

It recreates the awesome and unpredictable feeling of flight. But then, perhaps that description doesn't really quite do Z Force justice. Randy Geisler, president of the American Coaster Enthusiasts, says it best: "Z Force gives the sensation of dive bombing like airplane fighter pilots."

It is Top Gun all the way.

Peter Schnabel, executive vice president of Intamin, the coaster's designer, calls Z Force an extremely intense ride, pointing out, "We found that the varying pace of Z Force would help the riders remember the thrill feelings longer than if the trains traveled consistently as fast as other coasters."

Spurgeon Richardson constantly marvels at the amazing structure of the ride. He shakes his head as he says, "Z Force looks so incredibly compact compared to traditional roller coasters. This advanced creation is light years away from the bobsled-styled slides that were the first coasters. Z Force is the only ride of its type in the world. It is on the cutting edge of theme park technology of the 1990s."

Randy Geisler knows and understands coasters as well as anyone. He has ridden 280 of them, and he emphasizes, "Z Force rates as one of the most exciting that I've been on."

Roller Coasters have long tantalized those who want to experience the far edge of carefully controlled excitement. The first one was built in Russia in the 16th century, and the brave gathered to ride sleds seventy feet down a wood-frame ice slide in St. Petersburg. The French copied the "Russian Mountain," creating "Les Montagnes Russes," featuring wheeled vehicles that came rolling down large wooden ramps.

Force is the newest creation in innovative coasters.

79

In 1884, however, LaMarcus Thompson fashioned the design that ushered in the modern roller coaster era. He built the legendary "Switchback Railway" and placed it at New York's famed Coney Island. Those first riders were treated to a gentle journey at six miles per hour along a slightly-curved track. No one fainted. Only a few even expressed fright.

As time and technology moved quickly ahead, designers suddenly began including shallow dips and brightly-lit indoor scenes on their coasters. Soon they added speed. And by the 1920s, the Golden Era of roller coasters had finally dawned across the country. Within a decade, there were more than 1,500 of them in operation, and parks were competing to see just who could build the highest, the fastest, the most exciting ride known to mankind.

Nothing has changed.

When Six Flags Over Georgia opened in 1967, it had only one coaster-styled ride, the tame Dahlonega Runaway Mine Train that, aesthetically, sought to recreate the Georgia gold rush days. Of course, there was the Log Flume, always wet, always popular. But it simply drifted along through water-filled troughs, easing ever closer to that one final splash down, the only real breath-catching moment of the ride. It was gentle and slow paced. Yet the demand for the Log Flume became so great that Six Flags Over Georgia had to add a second one.

In 1973, however, the park signalled the new age of coasters when it introduced the Great American Scream Machine, a white, shining, replica of those old-fashioned wooden roller coasters from another time. Towering more than a hundred feet into the air, the Scream Machine is a genuine classic, boasting 3,800 feet of track. It has been named the nation's most beautiful coaster. And, the year it was built, the Great American Scream Machine was listed in the Guinness Book of Records as the world's largest wooden coaster.

That was only the beginning of the thrill ride craze that swept across the country and found itself a permanent home at Six Flags Over Georgia.

The Mind Bender is the world's only true triple-loop coaster. It carries you through those three loops—two of them vertical—at speeds up to fifty miles an hour.

Free Fall, some say, simulates the feeling of falling through space. Others swear that it is more like dropping from the top of a ten-story building.

Splashwater Falls lets you cool off rather quickly by plunging down a man-made waterfall. The idea for the Thunder River ride was taken from a kayak race course that was built for the Olympics in Munich, Germany. It is a churning and turbulent journey through unpredictable whitewater rapids.

And now comes Z Force and the thrill of a lifetime.

The peaks of the Blue Ridge Mountains
crown North Georgia with a rugged and spectacular beauty.
It was the land of the Cherokee.
It was streaked with gold.
Its canyons run deep, and the walls of the Blue Ridge
are splashed with the cascading veiled lace
of magnificent waterfalls.

Rock City
The View from the Top of the World

The land that begat Rock City was, more than anything else, a gift of nature, the wind-chiseled crown of a wild mountain range that sat perched on top of the world. The rugged, timbered slopes of Lookout Mountain knifed into the southern highlands and formed a forbidding wall more than a hundred miles long. It rose up with an unforgettable majesty for almost a half mile above sea level. And on a clear day, it was quite possible to stand at the summit of Lover's Leap and see across the landscapes of seven states: Georgia, Tennessee, North and South Carolina, Alabama, Kentucky, and Virginia.

Back in the mid-1920s, Garnet Carter found himself drawn to Lookout Mountain almost as though its peaks were magnets. Carter was a handsome, cigar-smoking optimist who had lost a fortune in the miniature golf craze of the Roaring Twenties. But he remained as undaunted as the high country around him, even launching a luxury home development for Chattanooga, Tennessee, and placing it atop Lookout Mountain. For a time, it prospered, then the Great Depression struck, and Carter realized he had real estate that no one could afford anymore.

His wife, Frieda, however, had become intrigued with the primeval beauty of those ten wilderness acres that overlooked seven states, and she laid out a pine needle path through the massive stone formations, referring to it simply as Rock City Gardens. She collected wildflowers and shrubs, indigenous to the area, replanting them along the primitive pathway. By 1930, Carter glimpsed the actual possibilities that Rock City offered him. It was indeed a spectacular world that everyone should see. But how would they learn about Rock City? He summoned a young aide, Clark Byers, telling him to persuade as many farmers as possible to paint advertising messages on their barns.

"But what would we paint on them?" Byers asked.

Carter scrawled three words on a piece of paper and handed them to his aide. All they said was: "See Rock City."

It wasn't long until there were more than 800 signs on barns in 18 states from Canada to Texas, and Carter and Byers became known as the "barnyard Rembrandts." But people read those messages, and they came by the thousands to see what Rock City was all about. None left disappointed.

Still they come to see the natural, awesome beauty that surrounds such charming exhibits as Mother Goose Village and Fairyland Caverns, grottos illuminated through the magic of black light, watching craftsmen at work in the Dulcimer Shop, squeezing their way through Needle's Eye, and passing Mushroom Rock, Cave of the Winds, and Goblin's Underpass on their way to Lover's Leap and the breathtaking sight of seven states.

Carter's great nephew, William H. Chapin, now serves as president of Rock City, and he carries on a time-honored philosophy: "Rock City has to be worth what a guest spends on it." But then, that's the way it has always been.

The view from Lover's Leap focuses on the landscapes of seven states.

Magic Carpets in the Land of the Cherokees

Dalton lies nestled in the cradle of the Blue Ridge Mountains, surrounded by natural beauty and interlaced with memories from a distant past. Once it was an integral part of the Cherokee Nation, a proud tribe, a learned tribe that was forced to jerk its historic roots from the valley and trek westward along a broken-hearted Trail of Tears.

The Cherokees left behind their hearts, all buried deep within the shadow of the Blue Ridge. They left behind the Federal style brick mansion of Chief James Vann. In 1956, the showplace of the Cherokee Nation was reclaimed and restored as the first project of the Whitefield-Murray Historical Society. Included in its collection are original artifacts and personal belongings of the Vann family.

Candy Ayers, manager of the city's Convention & Visitors Bureau, explains, "Dalton still holds to its Cherokee heritage by serving as a gateway to the new Chieftain's Trail."

The historical society, preserving records, artifacts, and landmarks of the area, is headquartered at Crown Gardens and Archives, an old cotton mill in Dalton. Other restoration projects of the society include the 1852 Depot; the home of Ainsworth E. Blunt, the city's first mayor and postmaster, a legacy from 1848; the home of Colonel W. C. Martin; and Prater's Mill, constructed in 1859 by slave labor.

Twice each year, on Mother's Day weekend in May and on Columbus Day weekend in October, Prater's Mill becomes the site of an old-fashioned country fair. The mill itself was built across Appalachia's Coahulla Creek from hand-hewn pine timbers. Powered by huge mill stones, it grinds corn and wheat during the fair just as it did during Georgia's rural days of the eighteenth century. Artists work with oils, water colors, acrylics, and photography. And craftsmen demonstrate such traditional handiworks as blacksmithing, spinning, weaving, and Dalton's own famous handtufted bedspread making.

Around the turn of the century, Catherine Evans, a young farm girl, sold a hand tufted bedspread for $2.50. Other women followed her example, and the popularity of the craft swept the nation. By the 1930s, machinery had been perfected to do the work, and the tufted carpet industry ultimately grew out of its bedspread phase, becoming a $5 billion business in Dalton. Other companies headed to the Georgia Blue Ridge, producing thread, yarn, textile chemicals, and machinery for tufting. Georgia's top industry remains textiles, and Dalton is known as the "The Carpet Capital of the World." It has more than 200 carpet and rug outlets, all open to the public, all offering 30 to 50 percent discounts.

The Dalton Convention & Visitors Bureau thanks Dalton Chrysler, Plymouth, Dodge; Days Inn; Realty World—Looper and Parks; Beckler's Carpet Outlet; Howard Johnson Motor Lodge; Walnut Square Mall; and Miller Brothers Rib Shacks for their strong support of tourism in Dalton.

Prater's Mill was built on land that was once part of the old Cherokee Land Lottery.

THE BIG A

Governor Joe Frank Harris was talking about the Greek Revival mansion in which he lived, the mansion that all Georgia governors call home.

"It has," he said proudly, "rare antiques, beautiful architecture, and lovely gardens. Georgians strive for the best and that is what you will find here."

He could just as easily have been talking about all of Atlanta, about every community tucked away behind every pine, within every hollow, of the whole state of Georgia.

The skyscrapers of the Big A stand tall at the edge of Piedmont Park in Atlanta.

6.

Margaret Mitchell gazed with a certain fondness and fascination upon the countryside around her. Then she sat down and wrote: "It was a pleasant land of white houses, peaceful plowed fields and sluggish yellow rivers, but a land of contrasts, of brightest sun glare and densest shade. The plantation clearings and miles of cotton fields smiled up to a warm sun, placid, complacent. At their edges rose the virgin forests, dark and cool, even in the hottest noons..."

It was also the land of her birth, her inheritance, for she had descended from people who had loved Georgia and fought for Georgia since the long-ago days of Revolutionary War.

Georgia is Margaret Mitchell country. She worked for a time as a feature writer on the *Atlanta Journal*. And it was here that she penned her 1936 novel, *Gone With The Wind*. In the heart of Jonesboro's Historic District is the courthouse where Margaret Mitchell came to research her tempestuous love story of Scarlett O'Hara and Rhett Butler, set against the flaming backdrop of Civil War. But then, in the book, the classical, white-columned manor of Tara lay only five miles away. Fayetteville's antebellum Fife House once served as the home for both faculty and students at Fayetteville Academy, attended in the novel by the fictional Scarlett O'Hara. The town even has the Margaret Mitchell Library, containing one of the nation's most complete reference collections which deal with the War Between the States, romantic, perhaps, only in the words of and in the mind of Margaret Mitchell.

The conflict left Atlanta lying in agony and in ashes, and its loss sealed the fate of the Confederacy. The battle is movingly remembered visually in a mural that wraps itself around Atlanta's Cyclorama. The sights, the sounds, the pain, the desperate acts of war are hauntingly captured with music and narration in an awesome creation that measures 42 feet in height, weighs 9,334 pounds, and has a circumference of 358 feet. The mural, painted in 1885 by German and Polish artists, traveled throughout the nation before finally coming home to the city whose destruction it commemorates. In *Gone With The Wind*, Margaret Mitchell describes the burning of Atlanta as "a screaming hell." Those who witness the mural know why.

The Swan House possesses the grace and the elegance of Tara. It symbolizes the best of old Atlanta, inspired by a style that flourished in England during the time of Queen Anne. The archives of its Margaret Mitchell Memorial Library provide an invaluable assortment of original manuscripts, newspapers, early maps, and old photographs. In the Swan House Civil War Museum, a wall map, a relic of the 1800s, depicts the major engagements of the Atlanta campaign, along with other memorabilia and artifacts from those long, hard days of fighting.

Out back, the modest Tullie Smith House is one of Atlanta's last surviving antebellum homes, weatherboarded and unadorned, designed in a "plantation plain style."

The gentle care given to historic homes around Atlanta has always symbolized Georgia's appreciation for its near and distant past. McElreath Hall houses an extensive collection that underscores the city's history. Wren's Nest was home of another renowned Georgia author, Joel Chandler Harris, who listened to the tales, the dialects of rural, backwoods folks, and pulled the wit and wisdom of Uncle Remus from out of their imaginations. On "Sweet Auburn" street, the memory of Civil Rights leader Dr. Martin Luther King, Jr., burns brightly at his birthplace, his tomb, and at the Ebenezer Church where he preached and pastored.

The Governor's Mansion, open for tours, has Neo-Classical furnishings, paintings, and porcelain from the 19th century, including a fine collection of Federal period furniture. Its library is filled with the priceless works of Georgia authors, such as Flannery O'Connor, Erskine Caldwell, Carson McCullers, Joel Chandler Harris, and, of course, Margaret Mitchell.

Decatur keeps its antebellum houses clustered quaintly in the DeKalb Historic Complex. Marietta has walking tours to the memorable homes of yesterday. And Roswell's Historic District of 1838 showcases fifteen structures that withstood Sherman's siege and escaped the burning torches of war.

They, too, could have all been gone with the wind. But they remain restored and unforgotten, never to be forgotten.

The Governor's Mansion captures the grace and the dignity of the state it serves.

A City of Vision, The Cornerstone of the New South

Atlanta was destined for greatness, even from that day in 1837 when Colonel Stephen Long and his engineers drove a stake into the Georgia thicket, marking the southernmost point for their new Western & Atlantic Railroad.

In time, a hamlet grew up around the wilderness tracks, and it was called, appropriately enough, Terminus. It became a city. It became the cornerstone of the New South. It became Atlanta.

Atlanta rose up as a major railroad hub, the Confederacy's primary warehousing center. That would also be its downfall. Atlanta burned, but only its buildings, never its vision, lay in ashes. No one could destroy its vision.

Atlanta was originally staked to the good earth to be a transportation center. And it has become one. The city's Hartsfield Atlanta International Airport, the world's busiest, handles 800,000 aircraft landings and 48 million passengers a year. And Atlanta, the international city, offers air routes to twenty-five destinations in fourteen foreign countries.

With two and a half million people, Atlanta has become the thirteenth largest metropolitan area in the United States, strong as both a tourism and a convention destination. In fact, the city now ranks as the third most popular convention and meeting site in the nation, behind only New York and Chicago. After all, it does have the Georgia World Congress Center, the country's premier exhibit and convention facility, as well as the Atlanta Market Center and the Georgia International Convention and Trade Center. And getting around town is easy via the integrated bus and rail system of MARTA.

Atlanta is proud of its many historic sites, including the Herndon House, the home of slave-born Alonzo Herndon who founded the Atlanta Life Insurance Company; The Jimmy Carter Presidential Center; and the Martin Luther King Center for Non-Violence. It focuses on culture at the High Museum of Art and on wildlife at the 40-acre Atlanta Zoo. And studio tours at CNN allow you to witness first hand the business of reporting television news.

The new city of the New South—the crossroads for I-85, I-75, and I-20—has 43,500 hotel rooms that range from comfortable budget accommodations to deluxe, luxury facilities. Twenty-five major downtown hotels form a dynamic skyline of steel and glass sculpture. The Westin Peachtree Plaza, towering 73 floors above the street, is the tallest hotel in the western hemisphere, and the Atlanta Marriott Marquis, with 1,674 rooms, is the largest hotel in the South. Two Ritz Carlton hotels grace Atlanta, offering European tradition and style. And, of course, there is the Hyatt Regency Atlanta, whose soaring atrium and revolving rooftop lounge launched a whole new architectural trend in hotels more than two decades ago.

Atlanta was indeed destined for greatness. And it has surpassed even the greatest of dreams.

The dynamic skyline of Atlanta rises above the remnants of its past.

A Changing
Image of the New South

DeKalb County is a startling, unexpected, and paradoxical kind of place, shadowed and sometimes hidden behind the thick pine and hardwood forests that still line its quiet, secluded streets. It is as Southern as grits and red-eye gravy, with a noble antebellum architectural and historic flair that has not gone with the wind. It strongly understands the importance of its past, yet DeKalb County dares to focus its vision on the vast opportunities that are beckoning in the future.

Perhaps that is why Decatur firmly believes it symbolizes a part of the South that few ever thought they would see. The town itself is old, dating back to the unpredictable days of 1823 when it stood virtually alone on the Georgia frontier. In fact, Decatur was already a prosperous, cultural community, as well as a major stagecoach stop, long before anyone ever got around to staking out Atlanta as an isolated, backwoods railroad terminus for the Western-Atlantic railroad line.

Downtown Decatur has the charm and antique aura of a small, out-of-the-way Southern town, with quaint shops and offices and restaurants all fanning out around a grand old granite courthouse. However, appearances are not always what they seem to be. Looks can sometimes be deceiving, and they certainly are in Decatur, a burgeoning city on the northern fringe of Atlanta that has become home for 300 of the Fortune 500 companies, as well as 160 foreign firms from more than twenty countries. The International flavor of DeKalb County is even more evident down at the sprawling Farmer's Market where Indians, Pakistanis, Thais, Laotians, Ecuadorians, and Ethiopians, as well as dozens of other ethnic groups, bring their aromatic wares to the nation's largest privately-owned food market. On any day, the tables are stacked with fresh produce from around the world, alongside a tantalizing variety of meats, cheeses, homemade pastas, and even flowers. It is an experience not quickly forgotten, nor does anyone want to forget. Throughout the year, DeKalb County further enhances its international reputation with a Greek Festival, Scottish Rite Festival, Olde English Festival, and Highland Games. And it just may be the only region of the New South that actually celebrates an authentic Chinese New Year. If it's not really expected, it can probably be found somewhere in DeKalb County.

The towering skyscrapers of Atlanta rise just beyond the treelines, on the southern side of the hills, leaving Decatur a wooded oasis amidst a contemporary and concrete world. It is a gateway to the outdoors with more than 200 tennis courts, a dozen golf courses, and twenty-two swimming pools. And not far away is frenetic Hartsfield Atlanta International Airport, the world's largest. The second busiest airport in the state, surprisingly enough, is even closer, the DeKalb-Peachtree.

Even though DeKalb County is perched squarely on the leading edge of one of the nation's top five metropolitan growth areas, Decatur reverently

The beauty of DeKalb County is framed by the dogwoods.

remembers and showcases the architectural artifacts of its historic and recent past.

Callanwolde is the magnificent Tudor-style mansion built in 1920 as the home of Charles Howard Candler, the eldest son of Coca-Cola founder Asa G. Candler. Originally the estate spread leisurely and elegantly across 27 acres of Atlanta's beautiful Druid Hills, created by the same firm that designed New York's Central Park. The sculptured lawns, formal gardens, nature trails, and rock garden have all been restored, and the 27,000-square-foot manor presently serves as the Callanwolde Fine Arts Center. At any time there may be dance performances, both classical and contemporary concerts, or even top drama productions going on within the walls of Callanwolde. And the home is always open for historical tours.

Time-honored remnants of the War Between the States are scattered throughout the area. The Swanton House, a landmark since 1823, was captured by Union Forces and converted into a command post when General William T. Sherman's Army from the North made its fiery march on Atlanta. The Biffle Cabin has also survived since the stagecoaches rolled through in the 1820s. And the Mary Gay House was the residence of the spunky Civil War heroine who diligently fed women and children while Sherman's siege tightened the noose around Atlanta and who later authored "Life in Dixie During the War."

The regal old courthouse, standing guard over the town square with cannons that once fought desperately to defend Atlanta, presents a broad range of exhibits and displays from the DeKalb Historical Society. It is a good place to study the harsh, everyday existence of the footsoldiers who fought the War Between the States. In addition, there is prehistoric pottery, tools used by early settlers, period clothing, and the assorted paraphernalia of an authentic railroad office.

But then, railroads have always played a critical role in the life and times of DeKalb County. When the storms of war raged into Georgia, Decatur served as a transportation center. And people hurried down to meet each train, eager for some news from the front. In time, the Union Army bombarded Decatur simply because it was necessary to destroy the tracks.

The present Depot was built in 1891 as Atlanta reclaimed itself from the ashes of conflict. Each Saturday, the New Georgia Railroad roars through the heart of DeKalb County, on out to Stone Mountain Village, and into Stone Mountain Park itself as it rumbles nostalgically around an 18-mile Atlanta loop. Old Steam Engine 750, which made its maiden run on the eastern coast of Florida in 1910, pulls eight vintage passenger cars as it chugs along, slowly retracing the storied tracks of Atlanta's turbulent, yet courageous past.

Romeo and Juliet is performed at Oglethorpe University's Shakespeare Festival.

A hush quietens the land where only the distant sound of a songbird disturbs the silence. A sense of tranquility and peace pervades an unspoiled, primeval

97

forest that surrounds the Fernbank Science Center, a unique museum and classroom. Its mission is far reaching: to entertain, educate, and promote a deeper understanding of science and technology, communicating the order and harmony of the natural world.

Fernbank's great exhibition hall interprets both life and physical sciences with displays that dramatically portray the natural environment and vanishing habitats of Georgia and the Southeast. The Okefenokee Swamp becomes a wet and trembling earth. Dinosaurs raise their heads above a wild, prehistoric landscape. And the geologic history of Georgia, featuring the reconstruction of a Saber-toothed Tiger, allows you to view the world with the eyes of an artist and understand it with the appreciation of a naturalist. Outside, a series of nature trails wind through the 65-acre Fernbank Forest, sometimes better known as the "school in the woods." It is the legacy of Miss Emily Harrison, a pioneer conservationist who wanted everyone to have—at least one time in their lives—an intimate experience with the wonders of nature.

At Fernbank, the sky is the limit as the center unravels the mysteries of the universe in one of the world's largest planetariums. Programs portray the marvels of the galaxies across a 70-foot diameter projection dome that is unveiled atop a 500-seat theater. The Fernbank Observatory gained national recognition for tracking the Apollo Lunar missions and for the live TV broadcast of Halley's Comet.

Emory University's Museum of Art and Archaeology is housed in a classical marble edifice that once served as the institution's Old Law Building. It features ancient art—prints, drawings, and sculpture—and archaeology from the Mediterranean, the Near East, the Americas, and Asia.

On view in the Egyptian gallery are a mummy dating to 300 B.C., three mummy cases, rare pre-dynastic decorated pottery from 3200 B.C., and an illustrated papyrus fragment from the Book of the Dead. Also displayed in the museum are Bronze Age artifacts from Jericho; objects from the ancient harbor of Caesarea, built by King Herod the Great; Greek pottery; and outstanding examples of sculpture from the Roman period.

There is an air of quaintness about all of DeKalb County. Stone Mountain Village, a nineteenth century portrait in the shadow of a giant and historic granite dome, offers the best in original crafts, antiques, art, and collectibles.

Chamblee's Antique Row has more than 30 shops in historic homes, churches, and stores, many dating to the mid-1800s. On display are American and European furniture, glass, pottery, quilts, primitives, tools, and architectural antiques. It is a place that wants you to know: "Old is beautiful; old is unusual; old is for today's living; old is new again."

But then, that can be said for all of DeKalb County.

Exhibits at Atlanta's High Museum cover a broad
spectrum of the centuries, from the Renaissance and the
Middle Ages to contemporary and avant-garde art.

The Monumental View of a World a Park

Everyone who looked upon the mountain of granite saw something different in its great stone face.

The Indians found two crevices atop a huge flat boulder that sat curiously perched on its summit. One ran north and south. The other cut east and west. And the Indians called them, with fear and superstition, "The Devil's Crossroads."

When the Spanish explorer, Captain Juan Pardo, marched through the country in 1567, he was amazed at what he called Crystal Mountain. It glistened in the sun. It even glistened in the glow of the moon at night. And Captain Juan Pardo was convinced that the great bald dome was surrounded with rubies and diamonds. They were so close. They glistened so brightly. But, alas, the Indians never let him close enough to pick any of the precious stones off the ground. It's just as well. They were beautiful but worthless.

In 1909, Mrs. Helen Plane, a charter member of the United Daughters of the Confederacy, gazed upon Stone Mountain and envisioned a Confederate Memorial carved deeply and proudly into the granite slab. Three years later, an editorial in the *Atlanta Georgian* was even suggesting that the world's greatest monument should be carved on the world's finest piece of stone. It was an idea that would not go away.

Stone Mountain stands 825 feet above the landscape and covers 583 acres. At least half of Georgia and part of North Carolina rest on the mountain's granite base. Its owners, the Venable family, deeded the face of the dome to the Stone Mountain Confederate Monumental Association in 1916 and gave the group twelve years to have its memorial finished.

When Gutzon Borglum saw the mountain, he had trouble believing his eyes. He was a sculptor, an artist who had gained national acclaim for his statue of Abraham Lincoln. And now he was being asked to carve some kind of memorial to the Confederacy on the largest, finest solid block of granite that had ever been placed in a sculptor's hands. All Mrs. Plane had in mind was a 70-foot-tall statue of Robert E. Lee. But Gutzon Borglum's imagination caught fire, then ran wild.

Upon the face of the mountain, he said, he would create an entire army on horseback and a cannon brigade led by the greatest of the Confederate leaders. It would have, Borglum boldly predicted, a cast of thousands. But then, he pointed out, the sculpture had to be massive since any small figure would be like sticking a postage stamp on the side of a barn.

In 1924, Borglum unveiled the head of Robert E. Lee, and a banquet was held for twenty celebrities who climbed down 400 feet of steps to dine on the width of Lee's shoulder.

It was a small triumph. It would be Gutzon Borglum's last. A personality rift developed between the temperamental artist and members of the

Stone Mountain Park is a unique world unto itself.

association. Then it widened. And Borglum angrily destroyed his models, packed up his sketches, and was gone, traveling north to South Dakota where he would carve the faces of Presidents on Mount Rushmore.

A new sculptor, Augustus Lukeman, proposed the classic style for a new design, one showing President Jefferson Davis, General Robert E. Lee, and Lt. General Stonewall Jackson on horseback. His deadline was now March 20, 1928. He did not make it. Lukeman, by then, had only finished the faces of Lee and Davis, roughly outlining the general's horse, Traveler.

The Venable family reclaimed their granite dome, and for thirty-six years, no one else touched the mountain.

The Georgia Legislature in 1958 named a new Stone Mountain Memorial Association, authorizing it to buy the ganite landmark. A new sculptor, Walker Kirtland Hancock, was chosen to complete Lukeman's design, and his changes were few. Hancock lowered the head and neck of Lee's horse so that more of Jefferson Davis could be seen, and he gave the President a civilian hat instead of the military campaign hat that Lukeman had put in his sketches.

The actual carving was done by a young foreman of the work crew, Roy Faulkner, a native Georgian, who had never had an art lesson in his life. It didn't matter. He was a genius at using the new thermo-jet torch to blast away granite and remove tons of stone each day. Faulkner knew that there was no way for him to erase or fix a mistake, so, for eight years, he hung onto the mountain and did not make any.

When dedicated in 1970, the sculpture on Stone Mountain was the biggest that the hand of man had ever put upon the earth, even larger than Borglum's faces of Washington, Jefferson, Roosevelt, and Lincoln on Mount Rushmore. The carving is 36 stories high and the length of a football field, so big, in fact, that workers could easily stand on a horse's ear or inside a horse's mouth to escape a sudden rain storm.

Historic Stone Mountain is massive. Mathematicians have estimated that if the exposed granite were loaded into freight cars carrying fifty tons each, the train would encircle the earth two and a half times. Legend says that old John Beauchamp bought it the first time, trading Indians forty dollars and a pony for the mountain. He turned around and sold it to Aaron Cloud for a muzzle-loading rifle, twenty bucks, and a bottle of raw whiskey. One man walked sixty miles to claim his land grant. But when he saw that most of his acreage was bare rock, he swapped his share of Stone Mountain for a mule to ride home.

However, it is more than a giant, gray, whalelike mound of granite jammed into Georgia's pineland hillsides. Stone Mountain today is a 3,200-acre park that blends an antebellum flavor of history with the rugged lure of the outdoors.

The sculpture on Stone Mountain is the biggest that the hand of man has ever put upon the earth.

103

Many believed that it had always been a perfect place for golf, nestled against a 400-acre lake among the trees. The problem, though, was that no one had ever played golf on a hard granite mountain before.

So Robert Trent Jones, recognized as one of the world's masters in golf design, was hired to develop the course. Some 300,000 tons of dirt were trucked in from another area of the park, and the solid outcropping of stone became thick, grassy fairways of hybrid bermuda. Greens are resilient Penncross bentgrass. And the rugged old mountainside suddenly got eighteen holes for an estimated $576,000.

Stone Mountain Park, sixteen miles east of Atlanta, has become a mecca for campers. Rustic campgrounds have modern facilities, including water and electricity. Various nature trails wind for more than twelve miles through the scenic and flora-accented country. One mapped trail even climbs for 1.3 miles to the top of the mountain, opening up vistas that stretch on for ninety miles. Along Wildlife Trails, elk, cougar, and bison—once indigenous to Georgia—can be seen in their natural, woodland habitat.

A heavily stocked lake, rimmed by a bank of granite, is home for bream, crappie, and catfish, and it frequently yields largemouth bass weighing as much as six to eight pounds.

One of the antebellum homes now restored on the Stone Mountain Plantation was headquarters for William T. Sherman on his 1864 march to the sea. When he left Kingston, Georgia, the general ordered most of the area burned. But for some unknown reason he spared the Kingston House, the manor of the Allen Plantation. Built in 1830, it reflects the Greek Revival architecture of the era. Scattered about the Stone Mountain plantation are several cabins, a country store, authentic flower and vegetable gardens, and the Thornton House of 1790. Many of the nineteen buildings were moved from their original sites in Georgia and have been authentically furnished.

A white paddle-wheel riverboat with galleried top deck daily cruises Stone Mountain Lake. An authentic, oldtime train chugs for five miles around the base of the mountain. The new Georgia Railroad connects the mammoth chunk of granite with downtown Atlanta. And Swiss-built cable cars offer a breathtaking view of the mountain and countryside during a four and a half minute ride to the summit of the granite peak. Nightly, from May through Labor Day, the north face of the mountain explodes beneath a dazzling laser show, a fantasy of color choreographed to the sounds of popular music.

The Stone Mountain Inn and Dining Room surround their legendary Southern hospitality with an elegant Colonial atmosphere. Robert E. Lee, Jefferson Davis, and Stonewall Jackson would feel right at home there. But then, in a sense, Stone Mountain is their home. As the editorial suggested so long ago, they will forever be part of the world's greatest monument carved on the world's finest piece of stone.

CLASSIC SOUTH

The early settlers of the 1770s had uneasily slipped into a territory purchased from the Creek and Cherokee nations, and the reports they sent back to Virginia and the Carolinas were indeed promising.

It was a good land, they said, a rich land, ''fit for the production of wheat, indigo, Indian corn, tobacco, hemp, flax, etc.''

That was enough. And the distant sounds of wagons could be heard coming across the Savannah River.

The aristocracy of the Old South was a
way of life on the wide verandas of its
beautiful homes.

7.

The classic face of a classic Georgia countryside is etched with tradition.

And beauty.

Elegance.

And antiquity.

The roots of Georgia are planted deep within its soil, for here a stubborn breed of men and women hammered together their first homes, harvested their first fields, taught their first schools, fought their first battles, and heard their first sermons of thanksgiving.

There was so much to be thankful for.

The little town of Louisville, in 1796, gained a certain amount of status as the site of Georgia's first capital. But a decade later, the seat of government was moved on to the trading center that James Oglethorpe had established on the river: Augusta. It came as no surprise. By then, Augusta was already on the verge of becoming a full-fledged city, even boasting Georgia's first academy, a resident theater, and a race track. Even the Presidential George Washington paid it a visit, and in 1806 the Parson Weems published a story in an Augusta print shop that turned Washington into a legend. He made up a little fable about the President who, as a boy, chopped down a cherry tree and could not tell a lie about it. Most believed the yarn to be truth. Only the parson, it seems, could tell a lie.

Louisville may have lost the capital. But it still has its Old Market downtown, built in 1758, and a cemetery which holds graves that were old when the Revolutionary War raged across its grounds, and the war raged far and wide.

Sylvania proudly keeps an eye on its Briar Creek Battle Site. And just outside of Washington, a band of Wilkes County men, led by Elijah Clarke, Stephen Heard, and John Dooly, soundly defeated the British at the Battle of Kettle Creek.

But the British took a measure of revenge. From their headquarters in Augusta, in 1781, they sent raiders back into Washington. Dooly was murdered. Heard's wife and child died from exposure in a snowstorm while their cabin burned. And Clarke's wife and children were also driven from their home. The Washington-Wilkes Historical Museum depicts the eras of conflict, and the Callaway Plantation complex, with a Greek Revival manor, log cabin, plainstyle house, smokehouse, barn, and cemetery, reverently focuses on the trials and triumphs of early American life.

One war ended, and peace spread across the classic face of Georgia. Prosperity rode the backs of cotton wagons from the fields. Beautiful plantation homes sat gleaming behind their great columns, as white as the cotton itself.

Then another war began. But not even Sherman's torches could destroy the antebellum luster of the countryside.

McDuffie County's Upcountry Plantation Tour leads past some of the earliest and finest homes in Georgia, all still looking with pride across the land of cotton. Alexandria was once the center of a large plantation in the early 1800s, an elegant Virginia-styled brick home. And the Rock House in Thomson, noted as the oldest documented dwelling in Georgia, has been restored as a house museum. Dating back to 1758, the stone dwelling is a reminder of the Quaker migration south.

Sparta's town square is surrounded by beautiful, antique homes, and its Hotel Lafayette, once known as the Drummer's Home, served as a haven for refugees fleeing scenes of battle during the War Between the States. Waynesboro's Historical Museum is located in a restored antebellum house. Sylvania's Dell-Goodall House was spared when an evangelist asked God to destroy the wicked town of Jacksborough instead. Greensboro is proud of its antebellum Greek Revival courthouse. Its past is vividly and poignantly recorded in the Green County Historical Society Museum. And Crawfordville has diligently placed its Confederate Museum inside the antebellum home of Alexander H. Stephens, the vice president of the Confederacy.

Augusta is crowded with grand, old, aristocratic homes. But then, Sherman didn't march on Augusta. Some whisper that he had a girl friend there. Or perhaps Augusta was simply out of the way on his march to the sea.

He left behind him tradition, beauty, elegance, and antiquity that remain unforgotten, never to be forgotten.

*The fabled elegance of the Southland
hides away within the historic
mansions of Athens.*

Augusta
An Aristocratic Home for Legends

The spirit of Augusta has not dimmed with the passing of the years. It was there at the beginning, even before the beginning, of Georgia. If fought valiantly for the land upon which it stands. It cast its lot with the soil, gambling on tobacco, then cotton. It prospered on the economic backbone of the farmer's almighty dollar. And it grew old with grace and dignity. Augusta, for all times, wears its age proudly, and it wears its age well.

Upon a timbered patch of rich, unplowed earth, down where the Piedmont Plateau clings stubbornly to the last vestiges of the Coastal Plain, General James Oglethorpe nailed together a fort, named it for Princess Augusta, and defied anyone to take it away from him. The French tried. But then, the French lay claim to all territory between New Orleans and the Savannah River, and they looked at Oglethorpe as an unwanted intruder who had no business leaving his footprints on the sacred soil of another's country. The general bristled. He was British, very British, and he and the band of settlers who had followed him to the outer edge of the Piedmont were proud of it. By the 1770s, they had all changed their minds.

By then, they were colonists, mad at England, and willing to allign themselves with a new nation and a new homeland they called Georgia. But, alas, the British flag was still flying above old Fort Augusta. So an American force under Lighthorse Harry Lee, Andrew Pickens, and Elijah Clark, in a major battle of the Revolutionary War, shot it down and raised a new flag, one with thirteen stars. And, in time, the fortress became a town, then a city, and finally a cornerstone of the New South.

Downtown Augusta, a rare and valuable antique, offers a sentimental journey through three centuries and six distinct Historic Districts.

Upon the original site of old Fort Augusta itself stands the fourth generation of St. Paul's Episcopal Church. The first one was built in 1750 and tucked away as close to the protection of the outpost as it could get. All that remains is the baptismal font brought from England in 1751. The present building was patterned after the 1820 church.

The St. John United Methodist Church was organized in 1798 by a young minister, Stith Mead, who spent his boyhood years in Augusta. But, unfortunately, he made the mistake of preaching a sermon one morning that strongly condemned the evils of life in Augusta. His congregation was startled, and the town was shocked. And the Reverend Stith Mead was never allowed to preach in Augusta's community church again.

The Former First Baptist Church is a fine example of Breaux Arts Classicism with a central dome and Corinthian columns. Erected in 1902, it replaces the revered building where delegates from southern states gathered in 1845 to form the Southern Baptist Convention.

Augusta nestles along the shoreline of the Savannah River. (Photo: Drake White)

110

Since the turn of the century, Sacred Heart, fashioned by Jesuit priests, has served as a spiritual and cultural center for Augusta. Beneath its towering twin spires and graceful arches, amidst its vivid jeweled tones of stained glass and carved Italian marble, Sacred Heart's great hall is now the scene of parties, lectures, concerts, art, and fashion shows.

The Holy Trinity Catholic Church, unfinished until 1863, heard the mournful wails of the grieving and the dying long before it ever heard a Sunday morning prayer. It was taken over by troops during the War Between the States and used as a Confederate hospital.

The First Presbyterian Church also had the unfortunate duty of trading a Bible for a scalpel, serving as a hospital during the war. It was designed by Robert Mills, architect of the Washington Monument and U.S. Treasury Building. And within its walls, the General Assembly of the Presbyterian Church of U.S. was organized in 1861. An early pastor was Dr. Joseph Wilson, whose son was Woodrow Wilson. So for a dozen years, from 1858 to 1870, the two-story brick manse became the boyhood home of the future President of the United States.

In fact, in a 1908 speech about Abraham Lincoln, Woodrow Wilson said, "My earliest recollection is of standing at my father's gateway in Augusta, Georgia, when I was four, and hearing someone pass and say that Mr. Lincoln was elected and there was to be a war."

$\mathcal{J}$t was a war that battered the face of Augusta, primarily because Augusta had become such an important cotton center. By 1820, the city ranked behind only Memphis as the world's largest inland cotton market. At the Victorian Cotton Exchange Building, along the riverwalk of the Savannah River, prices were quoted and duly recorded, and daily reports came in from throughout the United States and from ports as far away as Liverpool, England. It has even been said that great stacks of cotton, lining the sidewalks, were so thick that children could hop from bale to bale for the distance of a mile without their barefeet ever touching pavement.

Artifacts from the city's turbulent and sometimes chaotic past can be explored at the Augusta-Richmond County Museum. The building itself, erected during the reign of King George III, is Tudor in architectural style, with terra cotta drip mouldings, stucco, and battlements added during the 1850s. A decade later, it, like so many other proud, stoic Augusta buildings, found its rooms crowded with hospital beds, all filled with casualties from an unmerciful and uncivil war. Inside the museum, displays, murals, and dioramas trace the birth of a nation and Augusta's role in the bloody battles that stormed across its boundaries. There are also shrunken heads and intricate pottery from exotic parts of the world. And a Mikado Class steam locomotive with passenger and baggage cars links the city to its colorful era of railroading. At one time, in

Sacred Heart serves as a spiritual and cultural center of Augusta. (Photo: Drake White)

1833, the Charleston to Hamburg line, cutting through Augusta, was the world's longest railway.

Towering above Broad Street, an early center of commerce and trade, is the 72-foot high Confederate Monument, a tribute to the heroism of the Southern Rebel Army. It was commissioned shortly after the war by the women of Augusta who raised $20,000 to pay for the life-size carvings of Robert E. Lee, Stonewall Jackson, T. R. R. Cobb, and W. H. T. Walker, the city's own hero at the Battle of Atlanta. In Harrisburg, nearby, stands a 176-foot tall obelisk chimney, the last remnant of the Confederate Powder Works which manufactured 2,270,000 pounds of gunpowder during the conflict. And the final remaining column of the Old Slave Market can be seen on Broad Street. Legend says that a traveling minister was refused permission to preach in the market place. Enraged, he declared that the market would be destroyed and that every stone would fall except one. He swore that whoever touched that last stone would be killed. In 1878 a cyclone destroyed the building, save one pillar. Numerous attempts were made to move it. But the preacher's curse persisted, and each effort resulted in a man being injured. Now, no one ever tries to move it anymore.

The timeless dignity of Augusta is forever mirrored in its memorable houses. The Ezekiel Harris House, for example, was around in 1797, back when tobacco was the primary cash crop of Georgia. In fact, Ezekiel Harris had a warehouse to receive tobacco, and he advertised that planters could find lodging in his home, "a good frame house with a brick chimney." It is located on a hill overlooking Augusta, and it has the quaint architectural feel of New England.

The home of Mayor and Senator Nicholas Ware now houses the Gertrude Herbert Memorial Institute of Art. Lafayette himself even came to dance the minuet on its ballroom floor. The citizens of Augusta marveled at its elliptical staircase, ascending three stories, but they were outraged to learn that the mayor had spent the outlandish sum of $40,000 on his home. They would forever refer to it as "Ware's Folly."

Meadow Garden, built around 1794, was the residence of George Walton, a signer of the Declaration of Independence, a delegate to the first Continental Congress, and a governor of Georgia. The home is now operated by the Georgia Society of the Daughters of the American Revolution.

All three of the homes are open to the public.

Augusta has become known as the "South's Garden City." Its springs are ablaze with azaleas, and they drape the famed Masters Tournament golf course. It is a time when legends come to play. But then, Augusta is used to that. Augusta has always been the home of legends.

The charm of Augusta is mirrored in its beautiful homes. (Photo: Linda McFarland)

115

HISTORIC HEARTLAND

She walked slowly from house to house, her white hair glistening in the early sunshine, and she looked upon each of them as lovingly as she would her own children.

"They are the survivors," she said defiantly, then she smiled softly, "survivors of the late unpleasantness, although most folks don't refer to it as that. They simply call it the Civil War. But there wasn't anything civil about it at all. It was the war of Northern aggression is what it was."

The Fickling House symbolizes the elegant architectural heritage of Macon.

8.

$\mathcal{I}$t is a land and a time for the telling of stories.

In Madison someone is saying, "Sherman could have burned our pretty little town. But an old friend of the general's brother lived here, and he begged Sherman to save Madison. He must have caught the general in a good mood, because Sherman wiped out the cotton gin, the depot, and a clothing factory. But he left all these beautiful old homes untouched."

In Macon, the words are coming from the Grand Opera House. "This stage played host to such personages as Maude Adams, Lillian Gish, and Will Rogers. But I guess the greatest thing that ever happened here was when they set up treadmills and recreated the great chariot race from Ben Hur."

Outside of Eatonton, a man points to a huge rockpile and says, "It doesn't look like much when you're standin' here beside it. But from over on top of the tower, you can see that these rocks make the perfect outline of an Eagle with a wing spread of 120 feet. Some say it was built by Welsh explorers who arrived long before Columbus, and others tell me that it was built by a prehistoric tribe of Indians some six thousand years ago, probably for religious purposes. The whole thing is sure a mystery to me."

The stories are endless.

So are the grace and the charm of the Historic Heartland.

$\mathbf{T}$he gentle land—its legacy and its heritage—has always been an inspiration for the tellers of stories.

Sidney Lanier became the poet laureate of Georgia, and his home is part of the fabled, historic fabric of Macon.

Flannery O'Conner's country estate graces the landscape around

Milledgeville, Georgia's capital during the War Between the States. The Governor's Mansion there is regarded as one of the finest Greek Revival structures in the nation. And the old capitol building stands as imposing, as gothic as it did the day Georgians voted to secede from the Union.

Margaret Mitchell journeyed to Jonesboro to spend her summers on a grandmother's plantation, and the old farms, the grand manors scattered regally across the serene countryside gave her the idea for Tara, for *Gone With The Wind*.

And near Eatonton, Joel Chandler Harris, as a boy, would go down in the Mud Gullies and listen to rollicking folk yarns spun by the slaves. He wrapped up all of their tales and gave them to one man, wise old Uncle Remus, and Harris breathed life into Brer Rabbit and Brer Fox. A log slave cabin in Eatonton pays homage to his memorable menagerie of characters.

The stories are everywhere, mostly hidden away in a beautiful array of old homes, mostly Greek Revival, linked by the Antebellum Trail, a corridor of stately white columns that runs from Macon to Athens. The houses are reflections of an era when fortunes grew as high as cotton in the fields.

During the good life of those antebellum days, Madison was called, "the most cultured and aristocratic town on the stagecoach route from Charleston to New Orleans." A Historic District virtually encompasses the whole town, and its Madison Morgan Culture Center, housed in an 1895 Romanesque Revival grade school, features art galleries, a schoolroom museum, and a historical museum. Nine Historic Districts preserve Athen's architectural heritage, and many of the homes are tucked away around the campus of the University of Georgia, the state's oldest land grant college, founded in 1785. Athens even has a rare double-barreled cannon and an oak that owns itself.

Eight blocks surrounding Forsythe's courthouse square has forty structures on the National Register. Nearby Juliette's Jarrell Plantation portrays a century of farm life, showcasing a collection of 19th century houses, mills, and barns. Eagle Tavern in Watkinsville was a stagecoach stop that reveals the hardships and hazards of travel during the 1800s. Old Clinton has not changed much in appearance since its glory days, tied to the present by a dozen homes built between 1808-1830. And other beautiful homes nestle beneath the oak and magnolia trees of Conyers, Covington, Monroe, Barnesville, McDonough, Ft. Valley, and Social Circle.

The architectural stories they tell, the secrets they hide, behind their wide sweeping verandas and fluted columns, remain unforgotten, never to be forgotten.

Macon fought hard to stop the torches of Sherman and preserve the antebellum beauty of its architecture.

121

A Model of Elegance,
A Triumph of Good Taste

The dreaded and cursed William T. Sherman had been marching from Atlanta, headed toward Savannah, leaving the earth scorched in his callused footprints. But twice, his military forces were repelled in Macon, thus sparing a city that was too beautiful to burn. He left behind the culture, the elegance, the splendor of Macon's grand old homes as an architectural legacy of the Old South, white-columned reflections of one of the South's largest inland cotton ports.

But then, Macon, from its very beginning, was developed with an eye for beauty. When it was incorporated in 1823, its founders got together and designed the city with large squares and a myriad of parks, carefully following the blueprints of the ancient city of Babylon. It wasn't long before Macon was being hailed as the "Queen Inland City of the South." Its streets became lined with elaborate Italianate and Greek Revival mansions, with charming Victorian cottages, the handiwork of wealthy planters and businessmen.

Time has not changed the face of Macon. But then, neither did the Northern torches of Sherman.

Macon calls itself, with reason and with affection, the Cherry Blossom Capital of the World. In Spring, it even hosts an international Cherry Blossom Festival. And why not? After all, Macon nestles sedately beneath pink lace blooms that bind together the branches of 100,000 cherry trees, a glorious, positively breathtaking backdrop to the city's restored and revitalized downtown Historic District. Forty-eight homes and buildings have been individually listed on the National Register of Historic Places. Approximately 575 others have been listed for their architectural significance. Two are national historic landmarks.

The gracious living and antebellum elegance of Macon is best captured by the Hay House, built between 1855-60 by a highly-successful and diversified entrepreneur. He had raised millions for the Confederacy, and afterwards raised millions in Northern capital to rebuild the railroad that Sherman had destroyed. Legend claims that a secret room in the Hay House hid Confederate gold during the war. The Italian Renaissance mansion has 18,000 square feet on seven different levels, with such modern conveniences of the 1860s as hot and cold running water, intercom system, central heat and ventilating, and elevator. The twenty-four rooms of the Hay House, open for tours, are filled with priceless porcelains and antiques.

The Cannonball House and Confederate Museum was the only house in Macon hit by Union forces during the war. The Sidney Lanier Cottage is the Victorian birthplace of Georgia's best loved poet, who wrote "*The Marshes of Glynn.*" The Woodruff House was purchased by Colonel Joseph Bond who, in 1857, sold 2,200 bales of cotton for $100,000, a world record sale. And an 1884 editorial called the Grand Opera House, "a model of elegance...a triumph of good taste."

But then, that's what the essence of Macon is all about.

The Hay House is an Italian Renaissance mansion that mirrors the architectural splendor of Macon. (Photo: © 1986 Bard Wrisley, Atlanta, Georgia)

MAGNOLIA MIDLANDS

The farmer knelt in the fields of Vidalia and pulled an onion out of the ground, brushing the dirt off with the sleeve of his white shirt, stained by age and sweat.

"There ain't no onion like it in the world," he said simply, as though it were a fact that everyone understood.

"What makes it so different?"

"It's sweet, real sweet." The farmer grinned and took a bite. "It's just like eatin' an apple," he said.

*The mystique of the Midlands is found
in the Bulloch County Courthouse.*

126

9.

The settlers who ventured into the Magnolia Midlands cherished their land almost as much as their lives. It was rich. And diverse. It fed them. And gave them shelter.

For most, land was all that they had to call their own. They tilled it, toiled upon it, and depended on it. And land became the foundation on which to build a future. The land, they believed, was forever. It would never let them down.

Nothing has changed.

Land still preserves the vitality of the Magnolia Midlands. It was such a good fact, that Union soldiers, after the war, came back to found the town of Fitzgerald, only ten miles from where Confederate President Jefferson Davis was captured. A Blue and Gray Museum remembers the conflict and the years of healing. Those who found a home in the Magnolia Midlands have also found ways to celebrate the gifts that the land has given them.

At Vidalia, the soil and the climate conditions happen to be just right to produce onions, sweet onions, that have become famous throughout the world. And in May of each year, Vidalia holds its time-honored and internationally-acclaimed Onion Festival, even featuring a fresh-from-the-field Sweet Onion Cookoff and lip-smacking, no tears onion eating contest.

Down in Dublin, dirt farmers, as early as 1811, were bringing their corn by wagon to Chappell's Mill to have it ground into meal or flour. It was a necessity, a way of life, that became tradition. Not even time has stolen away the heritage of Chappell's Mill. It remains in operation, working hard beside the original dam that first helped the old mill harness the power that was generated by the waters of a seventy-five acre lake. Chappell's Mill grinds 15,000 bushels of corn a year, using a century-old grinding stone that was saved from destruction by Sherman's troops when they rode through the countryside in 1864.

However, it is at Soperton each November where the fine and respected art of milling grits from corn is showcased at the Million Pine Arts & Crafts Festival. More than two hundred exhibitors crowd beneath the evergreens to demonstrate and display work not unlike the handiwork of the 19th century. Making grits in South Georgia was an important art in those days. It still is. Not eating grits, some swear, is against the law, or at least it should be. The festival was inspired by the diligence of James Fowler, a forestry pioneer, who was committed to helping nature improve the land around him. For almost forty years, he trekked the area, planting by hand more than seven million pine trees.

Jesup depends on the water that spreads abundantly across the land. And fishermen, boaters, and water skiiers flock to its Altamaha River, Cherokee Lake, and Lake Lindsay Grace. McRae has water sports, as well as golf, tennis, and hiking trails at Little Ocmulgee State Park. Nicholls looks back to nature at General Coffee State Park, as does Reidsville at Gordonia-Altamaha State Park. And Statesboro rests peacefully and stately near the shoreline of the Ogeechee River.

Alma pays tribute to its gift from the land, annually hosting the Georgia Blueberry Festival in June. And Claxton, each March, honors an ornery critter that prowls the land at its annual Rattlesnake Roundup. Hunters collect hundreds of the poisonous reptiles, then milk their venom. Whoever catches the largest one gets a prize. And whoever catches the most gets a prize. It's not that difficult nor that dangerous, a wizened old hunter says. All you have to do is act like a snake, think like a snake, and move like a snake, only faster.

Claxton is also known for its world-renowned fruit cakes, a legend since the early 1900s. More than six million pounds of them are baked each year at the Claxton Fruitcake Company. But then, that should not be too surprising. After all, McRae is the proud hub of the Georgia pecan industry.

In Hawkinsville, the horses run. Standard breds are kept at the Harness Horse Training facilities from autumn until April. They compete in a weekend of classic racing at the city's Harness Festival, then the standard breds are shipped north for a season of racing at the nation's major tracks.

The land has indeed been good to the Magnolia Midlands. Its gifts, its legacy remain unforgotten, never to be forgotten.

Fishermen chase the elusive bass in the calm, beckoning riverways of the Magnolia Midlands.

Statesboro
A Legacy that is Sincerely Southern

A reflection of the Old South is mirrored in the proud, time-worn face of Statesboro. Its streets were once carved by the plodding, weary feet of horses hauling wagonload after wagonload of cotton from the fields, back during the early 1900s when Statesboro had the reputation of being the leading inland Sea Island cotton market in the world.

There were no warehouses in town. Farmers had no use for them. They would merely leave their horses tied up near the old watering trough, roll up their stained and dusty sleeves, and sell their cotton on the street. It was a grand era with money for everyone who had a little land and enough foresight to shove cotton seeds into the good earth.

The Jaeckel Hotel had been built in 1905 to take care of guests—from drummers to governors—who came riding into town on the Central of Georgia Railway. William Jennings Bryan even spent the night there before giving his famous "Prince of Peace" speech. And down at the Chautaqua, there might be an opera, a debate, or even a trained animal show. It didn't matter. Something was always happening in Statesboro.

Men would come from miles around to gather beneath the honored old walnut tree, long a Statesboro landmark, planted, some said, by Hernando de Soto himself when he came marching through the area in 1541. Indians had used the old walnut tree for a trail marker, and judges held their "Big Court" beneath its limbs twice a year. But mostly men gathered to fight or swap horses or talk politics and probably cuss General William T. Sherman who had had the gall to leave their courthouse and their land in ashes during his March to the Sea. It was the beginning of hard times. The dreaded boll weevil wrecked the cotton fields. And later, even the old walnut tree was dug up to make way for a new road. But Statesboro always fought back from adversity, and it never forgot the roots of its heritage.

The watering trough is still around. So is the Jaeckel Hotel. A historic country inn, the Statesboro Inn, offers bed and breakfast. The McDougald-Beaver House remains as a fine example of Neoclassical architecture. And the Holland House of 1892 shelters The Chatter Tree, featuring works from local artists and craftsmen. Both homes are open to the public.

The cotton empire died, but it was replaced by tobacco. Warehouses now echo the sing-song chanting of the auctioneers, and the fragrance of tobacco hangs heavy during late summer when those drying and golden leaves are brought to market.

Only minutes away, the wild and scenic Ogeechee River makes its way with unspoiled beauty toward the sea. It winds beneath the moss of aging cypress trees and through blackwater swamps, a perfect escape for canoeists or fishermen in search of redbreasts or stripers. And the historic remnants of nature can be found at the Georgia Southern museum, whose exhibits of Indian artifacts, fossils, and the skeletal remains of a 26-foot sea monster fully interpret Georgia's Coastal Plain.

The beauty of the wild Ogeechee River is captured at sunset. (Photo: John Powers)

PLANTATION TRACE

The old timer shuffled down the sidewalks of Albany, a wry grin on his face. "Back in the 1830s, they named this town for Albany, New York," he said. "They thought it would one day rival Albany, New York, in importance. After all, both towns were located on a river. One was on the Hudson. One was on the Flint."

"What happened?"

The old timer shrugged, and the grin began to slowly fade. "Boats could only travel up the Flint for twenty miles," he said. "The river played out long before it ever reached the sea, so that was that."

Pebble Hill Plantation is a gracious reminder of the glory days in Thomasville.

10.

Jt is a land of haunting beauty, with ghostly images rising up out of the shadows of the past.

They mirror a time when a man's wealth was as obvious as the white columns on his plantation home, when a hard scrabble life stained the logs of a farmer's backwoods cabin with sweat and tears that he cried alone, when the Indian had only the refuge of the woodlands, all he had ever wanted or known.

Sometimes only miles stood between them.

Sometimes they were separated by the centuries.

The Weeden Island people journeyed up the Chattahoochee River in 800 A.D., searching for a northern outpost. Their days on earth were numbered. Then came the Kolomoki Indians, carrying baskets of dirt, molding them into a giant temple, ceremonial plaza, and burial mounds. Their village ultimately became one of the largest population centers ever masterminded by a North American tribe. But by the time the 14th century dawned across Georgia, the nomadic Kolomoki people were gone, and their great village was only a ghost town, lying in silence upon the land. The remains have been pieced together at Kolomoki Indian Mounds and State Park, near Blakey.

As the 1600s ended, Spanish priests were trekking to their Indian missions in Georgia, cutting broad trails that became roadways for wagons hauling supplies into Lowndes County. The years have not erased their ghostly images.

Fort Gaines has the reconstructed replica of its old outpost, built originally to protect settlers from Creek and Seminole Indian attacks. And the city has collected abandoned, authentic log cabins from the region, creating a Frontier Village, portraying the pioneer development of the area.

For the pioneer farmer, his days were long and hard, and work was endless. His sometimes lonely, sometimes forsaken way of life is being remembered at the Georgia Agrirama in Tifton, the state's Agricultural Heritage Center.

More than thirty-five structures, commemorating the men and women who stubbornly coaxed their living from the soil, have been located throughout rural Georgia, moved in to the seventy-acre site, then faithfully restored. It is a place to better understand the daily chores that took place on a farmstead during the 19th century. Ham and bacon are curing in a smokehouse. Farm houses contain authentic furnishings. Craftsmen are making soap and quilts, and farmers plow the unpredictable earth. For costumed interpreters, it is a chance to pull up a rocker, sit a spell, and explain life as it was a hundred years ago.

The rural town at Agrirama is always growing, ever changing. Its streets are lined with a company store, grist mill, blacksmith shop, cotton gin, print shop, and sawmill. There are even rides available in an old logging train.

Agriculture has always played a savior's role in the history and the economy of those who walked the Plantation Trace. Ashburn and Blakely both have Peanut Monuments, saluting the peanut production in their individual areas. And Albany proudly proclaims itself to be the pecan capital of Georgia. The soil—producing such crops as cotton, corn, indigo, and rice—brought wealth to many plantations. During the War Between the States, Albany even gained fame as the "Breadbasket of the Confederacy." Its past is vividly captured in the Thronateeska Heritage Museum, the Natural History and Southwest Georgia Museum, and a Train museum.

Cuthbert has 34 homes on a historic tour. Vaidosta with reverence, shows off the architectural symbols of its wealth: the Barber House, built for the world's second bottler of Coca-Cola; Home of the Garden Center; and the Converse-Dalton House, a showplace from colonial times.

And Thomasville is draped with dogwood, crepe myrtle, and roses, especially roses. Its Rose test garden has almost 300 varieties and more than 2,000 plants. And a historic driving tour winds past the opulence of the 19th century when wealthy northerners were building their retreats and plantations in the winter resort of Thomasville. Classic manors, reminders of the era, include the Victorian Lapham-Patterson House and Pebble Plantation, a testimony to the sporting life in a home that is rich in both art and history.

The traces of their time on Georgia soil remain, ghostly yet unforgotten, never to be forgotten.

eorgia in the 1800s is interpreted by
ose who explain the lore, lifestyle, and
afts of another century at Agrirama.

The Perfect Crop that is One of Nature's Perfect Foods

If you drive along a Georgia country road, especially in the autumn, the chances are you will see peanuts. High in the timbered North Georgia mountains, the peanuts are likely to be boiling in a large pot at a roadside stand. Down South, they are in the fields, being harvested, or atop large wagons on their way to market. It doesn't matter where you may be, north or south, you won't be able to forget that Georgia is now and forever peanut country and proud of it.

Peanuts are the state's top cash crop, with more than nine thousand farmers growing peanuts on more than 600,000 acres. Georgia, in fact, ranks as the top peanut producing state, accounting for nearly half of the nation's supply.

From planting in April and May until harvest time during August and September, the peanut farmer's day is long. Most times, he's at work long before sun-up, and he doesn't quit until long after dark. But then, it takes hard work, as well as weeks and months of preparation and planning, to insure that Georgia peanuts represent the flavor and quality that have become an honored trademark of the state.

Most of the peanuts grown in Georgia are of the runner variety, known for their high quality and flavor. They are found in peanut butter and candy, used as cocktail peanuts. The climate and growing conditions in Georgia are a perfect combination for growing the runner variety of peanuts.

The job of taking the message of Georgia peanuts to the nation and the world belongs to the Georgia Peanut Commission, a farmer-funded organization that is responsible for research, education, and the promotion of the state's peanut crop.

Through cooperative efforts with similar organizations in other peanut producing states, the Georgia Peanut Commission has done its part in expanding the popularity of peanuts. The traditional peanut butter and jelly sandwich has long been enjoyed by kids from four to 94. Many top U.S. candy bars include peanuts or peanut butter. Cooks are discovering that peanuts are an ideal complement for delightful gourmet dishes.

The average yield in Georgia is 3,000 pounds per acre. The state thus produces about two billion pounds each year. And the per capita consumption of peanuts in America is eleven pounds per person. About half of Georgia's peanuts wind up in a jar of peanut butter, not bad considering that the average child eats 1,500 peanut butter sandwiches before graduating from high school. The rest of Georgia's peanuts find their way into candies, salted nuts, and various other uses.

Regardless of their destination, Georgia peanuts are "nutrition in a nutshell." Besides having 26 grams of protein, peanuts also contain B vitamins, fats, and a balanced share of calories. Peanuts have no cholesterol, and they qualify as a low sodium food. Both peanuts and peanut butter are acceptable for most diabetic, sodium restricted, cholesterol restricted, and some weight reduction diets.

Alongside Georgia's country roads, peanut farmers are hard at work.

ACKNOWLEDGEMENTS

The hard work, dedication, and professionalism of Bill T. Hardman and the Southeast Tourism Society who, for so long, have kept the travel spotlight shining brightly and successfully on the historical, recreational, and scenic attractions of Georgia.

Executive Director, Bill T. Hardman

President, Michael K. Smith, Marketing Manager, Biltmore Estate

First Vice President, Gary Stogner, director of public relations, Pinellas County Tourist Development Council

Secretary, Helen Fincher, manager, Augusta/Richmond County Convention & Visitors Bureau

Treasurer, Ansley Cohen, director of marketing, Palmetto Dunes

Vice President Alabama, Eva Golson, director of tourism, Fort Conde/City of Mobile

Vice President Florida, Suzanne McKenzie, co-creative director/copy chief, The McKenzie Group, Inc.

Vice President Georgia, Larry Allen, general manager, Stone Mountain Park

Vice President Louisiana, Preston Freidley, Jr., president, Shreveport-Bossier City Convention & Visitors Bureau

Vice President Mississippi, Vickie Thompson Miller, executive director, Jackson Convention & Visitors Bureau

Vice President North Carolina, Gail Story, national advertising director, Pace Magazine

Vice President South Carolina, Judy Knoechel, executive director, Columbia Convention & Visitors Bureau

Vice President Tennessee, Gene Lambert, executive director, Gatlinburg Chamber of Commerce

Vice President Virginia, Holt Maloney, director marketing & public relations, Luray Caverns Corporation

Past Presidents, Ed Stone, vice president marketing & public relations, Opryland, U.S.A.; Spurgeon Richardson, general manager, Six Flags Over Georgia; Terry Clements, director of tourism, Nashville Convention & Visitors Bureau

Board members: Roger Brashears, manager, Lynchburg Promotions, Jack Daniels Distillery; Bill Chapin, president, See Rock City, Inc.; Ken Carden, director of tourism, Jacksonville & Its Beaches, Convention & Visitors Bureau; Ronnie Kole, The Ronnie Kole Show; Lenore Barkley, executive director, Vicksburg Convention & Visitors Bureau; Randi Benner, divisional sales manager, La Quinta Motor Inns; Ken Boucher, district sales manager, Delta Airlines; Garry Bickett, director of marketing, Carowinds; Marcus Fields, president, Sky Valley Resort; Fred Ruder, vice president marketing, Mississippi Management, Inc.; Don Naman, executive director, International Motorsports Hall of Fame; Gary Greenhut, vice president & general manager, Savannah Convention & Visitors Bureau; Gerald Breaux, executive director, Lafayette Convention & Visitors Bureau; Miller Pope, owner, The Winds Beach Resort; Gary McCalla, editor, Southern Living Magazine; Patrick A. McMahon, director of tourism, Virginia Division of Tourism.